261.8 Sex as God Intended
McN

John J. McNeill

		DATE DUE	

SEX AS GOD INTENDED

A REFLECTION ON HUMAN SEXUALITY AS PLAY

JOHN J. MCNEILL

Foreword by Ken Page

DIOCESAN RESOURCE CENTER
1551 TENTH AVENUE EAST
SEATLE, WA 98102-0126

including

FESTSCHRIFT
ESSAYS
celebrating the life & work of John J. McNeill

Lethe Press
Maple Shade, NJ

www.lethepressbooks.com
lethepress@aol.com

Printed in the United States of America
Book Design by Toby Johnson

Published as a trade paperback original
by Lethe Press, 118 Heritage Avenue, Maple Shade, NJ 08052.
First U.S. edition, 2008

ISBN 1-59021-042-5 ISBN-13 978-1-59021-042-0

Library of Congress Cataloging-in-Publication Data

McNeill, John J.
    Sex as God intended : a reflection on human sexuality as play / John J.
McNeill ; including festschrift essays celebrating the life & work of John McNeill by
Mark Jordan ... [et al.]. -- 1st U.S. ed.
        p. cm.
    ISBN 978-1-59021-042-0
    1. Sex--Biblical teaching. 2. Sex--Religious aspects--Catholic Church. 3.
Homosexuality--Religious aspects--Christianity. 4. McNeill, John J. I. Jordan, Mark
D. II. Title.
    BS680.S5M39 2008
    261.8'357--dc22
                          2008040895

I wish to dedicate this book to Robert Galloway for his many years of unfailing support and encouragement and also to my students at Sunshine Cathedral who gave me invaluable feedback.

TABLE OF CONTENTS

PART 2

FESTSCHRIFT

FOREWORD

When I discovered John McNeill in 1991, a door opened in my life.

I still remember the fierce joy I felt when I was introduced to his writings. The God he spoke of was the God I'd been waiting for.

I was already out, working in the area of gay spirituality, but so lonely for this God of Freedom and Play who understood the connection between my gayness and my soul. John reminded me of ecstatic mystics like St. Francis or the Baal Shem Tov, the founder of Hasidism, which brought European Jews into the fields to sing and dance with God. So I sought John out, with no small amount of awe, and he has been my friend, mentor and spiritual director for all these years. John's teachings inspire me to hope, self-acceptance, and longing. His goodness is the basis of his greatness.

John's message may have evolved out of the pain of his life—but it culminates in a song of celebration. John lost his mother at age four, and grew up gay in Irish working class Buffalo, New York. He was a prisoner of war in Nazi Germany, and he came into the gay world when it was all shadows and shame. At a time when every authority told him that homosexuality was evil, he not only came out, he created a new theology of liberation. He had to cross a sea of self-hate and doubt in a boat made mostly of personal faith, against the authority of just about everyone he respected and trusted.

John couldn't come across in the ocean liner that so many of us can take now, with gay marriage, glossy magazines and gay consumerism. He had a choice: to fall forward into the despairing life the world offered gay people, or to fall backward into the arms of a God who delighted in him, gayness and all. His struggle brought him to the edge of suicide. During this time he had a revelation which became the cornerstone of his future teachings. He felt God saying to him "Don't kill yourself. You will be ok. You are ok. This very struggle will enable you to help others in the future." The message for him was that precisely where he felt most wounded, God would use him most powerfully. So he bucked the authority of theologians and psychiatrists, and "took a chance on God." In that choice, he opened up a portal for innumerable people to pass through. Those of us who don't have the fullness of John's faith have his to lean on.

So John began to build a vision of an embracing Christianity for LGBT people. And over the ensuing years, he watched his work attacked step by step by the Vatican. Cardinal Ratzinger, the man who is now Pope, dealt the final blow, completely severing him from the Jesuit community where he had lived and served for the last forty years. Providentially, this gave John the freedom to develop and articulate the fullness of his teachings without Church censorship. John says that gay liberation emerged out of the heart of the world for its healing. I say that John's message emerged out of the heart of gay liberation for the world's healing.

This revelation informs all his teachings; that at the heart of every struggle, every wound, is the blessing of God's privative presence. (Privation paradoxically signifies "presence in absence.") The experience of privation leads to a deep, painful longing for greater presence; in John's words, a homesickness for God. Thus John felt guided to seek out the places of the greatest pain in himself and in the world, and then to discern how the divine was manifesting exactly there. I've experienced this ability of John's many times. In our spiritual direction, I'd talk about something which was causing me pain, and when we were done, I'd feel a sense of God's presence right in the heart of my struggle. In my experience, John's insights are powerful because they are lit from within by his bond with Spirit.

I see John holding his sadness with a quality of sweet grace. He never stops leaning on God. He sees himself, in Henri Nouwen's terms, as, "a wounded healer." The capacity to take a chance on God is what has allowed John to come through such shame, punishment and loss and turn it into a breathtaking passageway of liberation for our community, transforming wounds into wisdom.

Another of John's gifts, so evident in this book, is his constant remembrance of the importance of authentic intimacy in human love and in our relationship with God. His insights have been a map out of sadness for me, through his nonstop reminder to choose love and community in my life. John brings everything back to the importance of human love. John's life is defined in the most central way by his relationship to Charlie, his partner of over 41 years. Having the love of Charlie is his major proof of God's goodness in his life.

When I was considering adopting a child as a single father, I was terrified, and wondered if I was mad to be taking on such a responsibility. John encouraged me—intensely—to follow through. My son is six now, and his presence in my life is a gift beyond telling. In the same way, John pulls us to real intimacy with God. He doesn't just teach us that God loves Gay people. He invites us to develop a radically personal relationship where we share our woundedness and our joy with Her/Him, allowing Spirit to heal our psychic trauma and fuel our love of life; an intimacy where we, too, fall backward into His arms.

John is not a proponent of "Spirituality Lite." The challenge in his work is what makes it so exciting. John says:

"When I think a thought and it makes my heart go aflame, when my heart burns with joy, anticipation and hope, then I know it is a message from God."

He challenges each of us to find our own message, a fierce and thrilling challenge, where the rubber meets the road. The choice to come out as our authentic self is often incredibly hard, and John kindly but bluntly challenges us to follow our own inner discernment over any authority. His uses of discernment are some of the most powerful psycho-spiritual tools I have seen in my years as a psychotherapist and spiritual seeker. Discernment occurs through noting the moments of emptiness and moments of fullness in our lives. As we connect the dots of what fills us and what leaves us empty, a picture begins to emerge, and it is the picture of our true mission. This process of discernment is what John calls "the complete democratization of spirituality," where each of us learns to hear and trust the place of "deep peace, quiet and joy," that signifies the presence of God. When I first met John, I was filled with desire to help gay men, particularly those who didn't follow any organized religion, to develop a living relationship with God. But my insecurities, the bone-deep experience of being the youngest child, the oversensitive one, the gay one, held me back, made me tentative in my expression. John saw what I was trying to do and kept reminding me that this was a mission of worth. His belief in me has been his most stirring gift. I see now, after working with so many other gay men, how many of us must fight that very same battle; claiming our tenderness and sensitivity as gifts of our soul, not sources of shame.

In this book, John explores the role of LGBT people in the world's healing around issues of sex and gender. John believes that each of us has masculine and feminine dimensions within ourselves, whereas the old heterosexist model tells us that we need only embody our traditional gender traits, masculine or feminine, and then look to the opposite sex to fill the empty dimension of ourselves. The queer revolution again puts the locus of revelation directly within us… the rich and constantly new permutations of our gender expression shift naturally between traditional masculine and feminine attributes. As we follow our own inner discernment, these attributes lose their titles, resolving into simply "self." And this is where LGBT people can lead the way... we have had to risk tremendous loss and even physical safety in order to honor our own sexual discernment. We have had to cross many trip wires of sex and gender taboo that heterosexuals may not have even noticed. And all of this is framed by John in the context of sex as play.

This is what I love most about John's teachings: their quality of celebration. His writing reminds me of *La Sagrada Familia* in Barcelona, Spain, the astonishing basilica that was the life work of the great Catalan architect Antoni Gaudí. As you climb to the top of this unfinished cathedral, you witness a dizzying number of scenes and images from the Bible. Ascending its long and labyrinthine stairways, you arrive finally at the top; wide open space all around. Nothing is dense anymore. The colorful and joyful spires at the top look like a child's fantasy, proclaiming *Hosanna in Excelsis* in exuberant script, past all theology... just a soaring song of celebration.

John's writings are rich with scholarship and insight, but what finally stands out is his God of Freedom and Joy. I welcome you to John's beautiful and visionary new book, with my favorite prayer of his:

God, we gays and lesbians are your special children. Grant us such a profound experience of your love that, healed of our wounds, we are free to play our lives in your presence.

Ken Page
Long Beach, NY 2007

SEX AS GOD INTENDED

INTRODUCTION

Christian revelation, as it came from Jesus, was one of the most sex-positive and body-positive religions in the history of the world. How, then, in just a few centuries did it become such a body- and sex-negative religion and remain so to this day? In the third century Saint Iraneus wrote: *Gloria Dei, Homo Vivens,* The Glory of God are Humans fully alive! That included being sexually fully alive. This is perhaps the central paradox of Christian history. As Hegel once wrote: "The Owl of Minerva unfolds her wings only at the falling of dusk." His point was that we can understand a civilization, a period of history or an institution only at its dying stage. It is my belief that Christianity in its present form is dying, along with all the major forms of Patriarchy representing the domination and suppression of the feminine by the masculine. The only way it can be resurrected is to recover and affirm the feminine, which will allow the Church once again to proclaim the body- and sex-positive message revealed by God. In a lecture in Hyde Park a man in his audience called out to G. K. Chesterton, "Don't you know that after two thousand years Christianity has failed"? "On the contrary," Chesterton replied, "It has not been tried yet!" This certainly is true in the area of sexuality.

THE USE OF SCRIPTURE

How did God intend us humans to use God's gift of sexuality? There are two primary sources we can use to try to answer that question. The first primary source is Scripture, the Old and the New Testaments. What did God reveal about God's intentions for human sexuality in Scripture? In the document from the Second Vatican Council, The Dogmatic Constitution on Divine Revelation, we are warned that we cannot make a simplistic conclusion from the translated words of Scripture without some scholarly knowledge of the background of the passage:

> Since God speaks in sacred Scripture through men in a human fashion, the interpreter of sacred Scripture, in order to see clearly what God wanted to communicate to us, should carefully investigate what meaning the sacred writers really intended, and what God wanted to manifest by means of their words. (*The Documents of Vatican 11*, ed. Walter M. Abbott, S.J. (New York: American Press, 1966).

We are fortunate to live in an age where scriptural scholarship has made that meaning more available to us than any time in the past 2000 years.

Whenever Scripture deals with sexual issues we must use what feminist scholars call "a hermeneutic of suspicion." Very frequently these passages have been mistranslated to meet the prejudice of the translator. We will deal with several such passages.

The Use Of Personal Experience

The second primary source we have to try to discern God's will for human sexuality is our own experience. At the Last Supper, Jesus promised to send every one of us his Holy Spirit who would dwell in our hearts and lead us into all truth. Each of us, then, have direct access to the knowledge of God's will for us through the Spirit dwelling in our hearts. This has lead to the ancient Christian practice of discernment of spirits. This practice presupposes that we have made a commitment to try to live in as close a union with God's Spirit as possible. God speaks to us through our hearts, that is to say, through our emotions. If we place an action in harmony with Christ's indwelling Spirit we will experience deep peace and joy. On the contrary, if we place an action that separates us from the indwelling Spirit of God, we will know anxiety and depression. Thus there is a direct feedback to us in all our actions, including our sexual activity, which helps us to discern what is or is not in harmony with the Spirit of God dwelling in our hearts.

Consequently, we have this two-pronged approach to help us answer the question what is God's plan for human sexuality. The first is a search, with the help of scriptural scholars, for what God has revealed through the sacred authors of Scripture about human sexuality. The second is by a prayerful discernment of what the Spirit of God dwelling in our hearts is telling us directly through our experience. Where there is a correlation between what we learn from Scripture about God's plan and what our personal experience is telling us, then we have the closest we can come to certainty about God's purpose for our sexuality.

What The Old Testament Says About Human Sexuality

What we can learn from Genesis

The Eloist Version of Creation

Most readers of the Bible are not aware that there are two distinct versions of creation in the pages of Genesis which give two very different interpretations of God's purpose in creating humans as sexual. Both accounts agree in seeing human sexuality as good. "God saw all he had made, and indeed it was very good" (Gen 1:31). The first account (Gen: 1 and 2; 4), is from the Priestly tradition and refers to God under the name Elohim. This tradition reads back into the creation account the special procreative covenant that God made with his chosen people, Israel. "So God created man in his

own image, in the image of God he created him, male and
female he created them." (Gen1:27). This statement has led
to a century old dispute as to whether the image of God is to
be found in the individual as such or can only be found in
the male and female united in marriage. (I will deal with this
dispute in my chapter dealing with the dialectic between the
masculine and the feminine in history.)

This account clearly indicates that the divine purpose
in creating sexual differentiation was procreation. The
first covenant recorded in the bible that God made with
humanity was a procreative covenant between God and his
chosen people. "And God blessed them and said to them: "Be
fruitful and multiply and fill the earth and subdue it…" God
promised his chosen people that if they kept the procreative
covenant, from among their descendents would come the
Messiah.

We should keep in mind the pro-fertility bent of the
Old Testament authors was due to under-population, with
the result that any willful destruction of viable seed such as
masturbation was looked on as a serious crime. Masturbation
had the same significance and moral weight in the Old
Testament as abortion does today. The seed emitted by the
male was thought to contain a fully formed human being.
The female was understood as a purely passive receptacle for
the male seed. Another factor influencing the Old Testament
understanding of homosexual activity was the strong Hebrew
stress on preserving the family name through progeny. In
fact, participation in God's covenant with the chosen people
depended on having children. One of the worst curses
that could befall a Jewish male was sterility. In most of the

Old Testament there was little or no emphasis on personal immortality. That will change dramatically with Isaiah.

Thus it was the sacred duty of every Jewish male to marry and have as many children as possible. In fact, in Deuteronomy, there is an explicit exclusion from the people of God of any male who became a eunuch. "A man whose testicles have been crushed or whose adult male member has been cut off must not be admitted to the assembly of Yahweh." (Deut: 23:2). It is evident that from a Christian perspective this procreative covenant came to an end with the birth of Jesus, the Messiah. In fact, in the Acts of the Apostles, the account of the baptism of the Ethiopian Eunuch was a clear revelation that all those who are sexually different and cannot procreate have a special place in the new covenant community.

The Yahwist Version of Creation

The second account of creation contained in Gen 2:5 and the rest of the chapter attributed to the author who refers to God as Yahweh is much more ancient, dating back to 950 B.C. In this account God's purpose in creating sexual differentiation is not associated with procreation; rather, the purpose was companionship and a cure for loneliness. "Then the Lord God said: 'it is not good that the man should be alone. I will make him a helper fit for him.' " Or to bring the translation up to date: "It is not good that a human be alone. Every human needs a companion of his or her own kind!" There is no mention in this account of procreation, thus, mutual love and fulfillment is equally a biblical norm for human sexuality. This second norm allowed Christian marriage to take place between two humans incapable of procreation. Christian tradition tended over the centuries to subordinate this purpose to the procreative purpose, making procreation primary and companionship secondary. It was not until Vatican II in 1966 that the Catholic Church recognized the companionship purpose as coequal with procreation. This purpose can be fulfilled in a gay or lesbian sexual relationship.

PUTTING HUMAN SEXUALITY IN HUMAN HANDS FOR HUMAN PURPOSES

Surprisingly, the primary message of the Old Testament concerning human sexuality was an effort to secularize human sexuality, i.e. separate our sexuality from divine worship and place it in human hands for human purposes. The pagan religions that were contemporary with Judaism used human sexuality as a part of divine worship. The pagan gods and goddesses were thought of as sexual beings who wanted to be worshipped in sexual ways. Most temples had their sacred prostitutes, male and female. It was believed that by having sex with the sacred prostitute, one gave pleasure to the god or goddesses and would be granted the blessing one requested. The primary expression of this belief was in fertility worship. Orgies were held in the fields to seek the blessing of rain. The maypole around which the celebrants danced was usually a phallic symbol. There is a continuous polemic in the Old Testament by the Yahwist author against this kind of fertility worship. For example, Exodus 32 tells the story of the Israelites turning back to idol worship and fertility rites while Moses is on Mount Sinai receiving the Ten Commandments from Yahweh. They molded an idol of a golden calf from their jewelry. Notice that the idol they worshiped was an animal. Fertility worship usually involved dehumanizing sexual activity and returning it to the depersonalized animal level, much as Playboy tries to reduce women to animals by having them wear bunny costumes. Their animal identity frees their sex partners of any human restraints. "And so, early the next day they offered holocausts and brought communion sacrifices, then all the people sat down to eat and drink, and afterwards got up to amuse themselves (Exodus 32: 6)." At that moment, Moses descended from Mount Sinai with the Ten Commandments, the first of which read: "I am the Lord, your God. You shall not worship any other God." When Moses saw their fertility rite going on, in fury he smashed the stone tablets of the Ten Commandments. Moses then called on the Levitical priesthood to punish the people for idol worship and, we are told, three thousand were killed.

Noah And His Sons

The theme of fertility worship occurs again in the story of Noah and the flood. Peter Ellis in his book *The Yahwist: The Bible's First Theologian* offers an interesting and suggestive thesis. The story of the flood is immediately preceded by a reference to the "sons of God lusting after the daughters of men."

The Yahwist's audience would certainly recognize in the story an illusion to the belief of the Canaanite religion that by means of sacred prostitution—sexual intercourse with male and female prostitutes at the Canaanite shrines—it was possible to enter into special relationship with the god or goddess represented by the sacred prostitute.

In the punishment, which flows from the fornication of the sons of God with the daughters of men, the rains come with a vengeance. The floods cover the earth, and everything on its fertile surface is swept away by cleansing waters.

One aspect of the story of the flood throws a strong light on the Jewish people's attitude toward homosexuality. According to J. Edgar Brun, the ultimate "that" of the wrongness of homosexual activity in Israelites' eyes can best be discerned in the account of Noah and his sons after the flood (Gen. 9:18-27). The present text states that after the first grape harvest Noah got drunk and was lying naked in his tent. His son Ham came in "and looked at his nakedness." It is obvious by what follows that Ham's sin involved something more than just a violation of modesty of the eyes. The second part of that story has obviously been expurgated and revised. The Hebrew of the text makes it quite clear that Ham did not merely look at his father but actually did something to him. Yet although Ham was the wrongdoer, Canaan, his son, is the person cursed. Brun believes the story was undoubtedly an anti-Egyptian polemic and searches to reconstruct it with an episode in the Egyptian epic entitled *The Contending of Horus and Seth* (XL:3-4)

Horus was the posthumous son and heir of the God Osiris, the primordial king and giver of life. He was invited by his uncle Seth to spend a day. Seth's real motive was not to show him hospitality but to disqualify him from inheriting his father's royal power. To this end, Seth got Horus drunk; while Horus slept Seth committed an act of sodomy upon him. Since sodomy was inflicted on a defeated enemy and was a symbol of domination, Seth could then claim that he had conquered Horus and demand the kingship in his place.

Brun claims that the original biblical story followed the same line: "By committing sodomy on his father who was the ancestor of all men after the flood… Ham (Egypt) could also claim the right to dominate all mankind." (J Edgar Brun, "Old Testament History and the Development of a Sexual Ethic," The New Morality (Philadelphia: Westminster Press). The revision, which omits any explicit reference to a sexual act and makes Canaan the recipient of Noah's curse, was prompted by the fact that the Canaanites had become the immediate threat to Israel's political and religious survival. Brun notes that the Jewish retelling of the story reverses the original judgment of the Egyptian story. Ham (Canaan) who commits the sodomy, instead of winning dominion, is condemned to roam the earth as a nomad and never have any dominion whatsoever.

The Egyptian pharaoh, when he sat on his throne, put his feet on a footstool on which were carved representatives of all the tribes the pharaoh had conquered. The official wording on that footstool for the Pharaoh's dominion was that "The Pharaoh has anally penetrated his enemies." During their captivity in Egypt, Egyptian soldiers systematically sodomized every adult Jewish male as an expression of contempt, scorn and domination. The same practice of anally sodomizing captives continues today amid nomad tribes in the Near East. The most famous case is that of Lawrence of Arabia.

Brun suggests that the principal reason the Israelites regarded homosexual practices as an abomination was that "They too viewed sodomy as an expression of scorn, where the dignity of the male was a primary consideration, voluntary acts of a homosexual nature could not be tolerated. Both parties would then be undermining the very foundation of a patriarchal society; the one because he uses another as a woman; the other because he allows himself to be used as a women. The dignity of the male is dishonored by both."

This understanding led to the law in The Holiness Code: "If any man uses another man as a woman, let them both be put to death!" Notice that if the sodomy was an act of rape, both the perpetrator and the victim would be executed. It is obvious too that the law is not based on a moral judgment on same sex activity. There is no law condemning same sex acts between two women. And there is no law condemning a sexual act between two men who intend that act to be an expression of love and affection. The next law condemns any woman who has sex with an animal to be put to death. We must remember that all the Patriarchs had harems. King David is recorded as having a thousand wives. There is no condemnation if these women took care of each other's sexual needs.

This means that the primary reason for the strong condemnation of homosexuality in the Old Testament was the presumption of male superiority and contempt for everything feminine and had nothing to do with a moral judgment against same sex activity. A famous Jewish prayer to be recited daily by every male was: "Thank God I was not born a woman." Consequently, the deepest root of the homophobia of the Old Testament is *feminaphobia*, a profound fear and contempt of all things feminine. The most important cure for this form of homophobia, which still exists today, is women's liberation to a full and equal stature with men in human society, a liberation that has been strongly in process for the past fifty years.

Sodomy

In July 2003, the Supreme Court of the United States struck down all sodomy laws on the books in the United States against the protests of most conservative church institutions. The lesbian and gay community responded with relief and gratitude for its liberation from 2000 years of unjust legal persecution. Thus, a secular institution, rather than the Church, finally achieved justice and showed compassion for persecuted gay people. The single most important factor in the Western Christian tradition condemning homosexual practices and leading to two millennia of persecution and suffering of the gay minority was the false interpretation given to the Sodom and Gomorrah story (Gen 19:4-11). The Institutional Church taught, and people universally believed, on what they held to be excellent authority, that homosexual practices had brought divine vengeance upon the cities of Sodom and Gomorrah, and that the repetition such "offenses against nature" had from time to time provoked similar visitations of divine wrath in the form of earthquakes, floods,

famine, plagues, war, etc. It was taken for granted that the
sin for which the seven cities of the plain were destroyed was
the habitual indulgence of perverse homosexual practices,
especially anal penetration, among men. This gave the
civil state the right and obligation to pass laws making all
homosexual activities illegal in order to protect the state
against God's just judgment. This was a primary factor in
transforming the Christian understanding of God into a god
of fear more like Baal than the Christian revelation of a God
of love.

What was the sin of Sodom and Gomorrah and what did
God intend to reveal about human sexuality in this story?
Two primary themes of the Yahwist author of Genesis are
intertwined in this narrative. The first of these themes has
to do with the virtue of hospitality and the second has to do
with the Yahwist polemic against fertility worship.

For an understanding of the development of the Sodom
and Gomorrah story it is important to place it in the context
of the legends of a similar character from the same period.
Many of these legends tell of a stranger (sometimes a divine
being in disguise) who visits a prosperous city and is refused
hospitality. He eventually finds lodging, often with poor
outcasts. Consequently, he helps his hosts escape before the
city and its inhabitants are destroyed. The most famous of
these legends is Ovid's account of Philemon and Baucis. These
legends account for the particular form the Sodom story itself
assumed during the course of its oral transmission prior to
being written down. The conduct which brings judgment
upon the offending community is never specifically sexual,

but always wickedness in general, and, in particular, pride and inhospitality.

Throughout the Old Testament, Sodom is referred to as a symbol of utter destruction occasioned by sins of such wickedness as to merit exemplary punishment. However nowhere in the Old Testament is that sin identifies explicitly with homosexual behavior. In Ezekiel 26, 40-50, we read: "Behold! this was the sin of your sister Sodom, she and her daughters (there were seven cities of the plain that were destroyed) lived in pride, plenty and thoughtless ease; they supported not the poor and the needy, they grew haughty, and committed abominations before me; so I swept them away, as you have seen."

A confirmation of the interpretation of the primary sin of Sodom and Gomorrah as inhospitality occurs in the teaching of Jesus in the New Testament (Lk, 10:10-13) where Jesus is recorded as discussing the problem of the inhospitable reception of his disciples: "But whenever you come to a town and they do not welcome you, go out into the open streets and say: The very dust of your town that sticks to our feet we wipe off in protest. But understand this: The Kingdom of God is at hand! I tell you, on that day Sodom will fare better than that town!"

Jesus clearly understood the sin of Sodom was inhospitality to the stranger. A negative proof occurs by that fact that wherever so-called homosexual acts are condemned there is never any mention of Sodom and Gomorrah

Prior to the story of Sodom in Genesis, a passage dealing with Abraham, the biblical author insists on the importance of hospitality in winning God's favor. When the angelic messengers are on their way to deliver judgment on Sodom, they pass Abraham's tent at an oasis in the desert. The quality of Abraham as a good man worthy of God's blessing is dramatically established by his hospitable reception of the strangers.

Raising his eyes, he saw three men standing near him. On seeing them, he ran from the door of his tent to meet them, and bowing to the ground said: "Oh Sirs, if perchance I find favor with you, please do not pass by without stopping with your servant. Let a little water be brought to wash your feet, and stretch yourselves out under the tree, while I fetch a bit of food that you may refresh yourselves. Afterwards you may proceed on your way, since you will have paid your servant a visit." (Gen. 18:1-5)

It should be noted that the hospitality to a stranger in the desert could easily be a matter of life and death. Because of Abraham's hospitality, the angelic strangers bless his wife Sarah with fertility, although she is already ninety years old. The clear message of this passage is that God blesses those who are hospitable to strangers with fertility. Human works of compassion and mercy bring God's blessing but acts of fertility worship of idols brings with it divine punishment.

FERTILITY WORSHIP

This brings us to the second strand of the Sodom story, the condemnation of pagan fertility rites. The quality of Lot, Abraham's relative in Sodom, as a good man worthy of God's favor is established in contrast to the other inhabitants of Sodom by his hospitality to the same strangers, in terms strongly reminiscent of the story of the disciples of Emmaus in John's gospel.

The two angels arrived in Sodom in the evening while Lot was sitting at the gate of Sodom. When Lot saw them he rose to greet them, bowing his face to the ground and saying: "If you please, Sirs, come over to your servant's house to pass the night and wash your feet." But they said: "No, we will pass the night in the open." He pressed them so strongly, however, that they went over to his house, where he prepared a feast for them, and baked unleavened bread for them to eat. (Gen. 19:1-3)

At this point in the narrative the second strand in the story begins, the condemnation of fertility worship. The Sodomites surround Lot's house and demand that Lot "bring them (Lot's visitors) out to us that we may know them!" Remember that these strangers are referred to as angelic visitors. We have a strong suggestion here that the Sodomites are involved in fertility rites and wanted to use the angelic visitors as temple prostitutes. That we are not dealing with homosexuality, same sex activity here is made patently clear by Lot's response to the Sodomites: "Please, my friends, be not so depraved. I have two daughters who have never had intercourse with a man. Let me bring them out to you that you may do with them what you will; only do nothing to these men, inasmuch as they have come under the shelter of my roof." (Gen. 19:7-8)

There are two convictions in Lot's speech. The first is the absolute sacredness of the guest (the law of hospitality) and the absolute dignity of the male sex to the point were the honor and the life of the women of the family are regarded as expendable.

THE CRIME OF GIBEAH

In the account of the crime of Gibeah in the Book of Judges (19: 1-21, 25), the inhabitants of Gibeah make an identical request of the stranger visiting the town. In this instance, however, the stranger releases his female consort to the crowd, and they so misuse her sexually that the stranger finds her dead on the threshold in the morning. At a consequent gathering of the tribes of Israel, the stranger makes clear what the crime of Gibeah was:

"To Gibeah, which belongs to the Benjamin, I came with my consort to spend the night; but the citizens of Gibeah rose against me. Me they intended to kill, and my consort they ravished, so that she died." (Judg.20:4-6)

In the crime of Gibeah, not only was sexual rape involved, but also the design to murder the stranger. As punishment for this crime, Yahweh called on the other tribes of Israel to wipe the tribe of Benjamin off the face of the earth.

The story continues that the angelic visitors protected Lot and the next morning ordered him and his family to leave the city. The prayers for rain were answered by Yahweh with a rain of fire and brimstone which destroyed all life and left the area infertile for ever. When Lot's wife looks back, she is transformed into a pillar of salt, another symbol of infertility.

PHILO'S INTERPRETATION OF SODOM AND GOMORRAH

The first writings to identify the sin of Sodom with homosexual practices in general—the writings which probably had the most decisive influence on early Christian tradition—were those of Philo, dating from the middle of the first century A.D. and those of Josephus from around the year A.D. 96. The first recorded instance of a homosexual coitus connotation being clearly attributed to the Hebrew word *yadha*, "to know" in the text from Genesis occurs in Philo's *Quaet. Et Salut*. In Genesis V: 31-37where *yahda* is interpreted as "servile, lawless, and unseemly pederasty." The association of the wickedness of Sodom with the lawlessness of the Gentiles has become identified with the pederasty of Greek culture.

In his work *De Abrahamo*, Philo reads all the evils of first century Alexandria back into the story of Sodom:

> The land of the Sodomites was brimful of innumerable iniquities, particularly such as arise from gluttony and lewdness…. The inhabitants owed this extreme license to the never-failing lavishness of their sources of wealth…. Incapable of bearing such satiety… they threw off from their necks the law of nature, and applied themselves to deep drinking of strong liquor and dainty feeding and forbidden forms of intercourse. Not only in their mad lust for women did they violate the marriages of their neighbors, but also men mounted males without respect for the sex nature which the active partner shares with the passive, and so when they tried to beget children they were discovered to be incapable of any but a sterile seed.

Yet the discovery availed them not, so much stronger was
the force of their lust, which mastered them, as little by
little they accustomed those who were by nature men
to play the part of women, they saddled them with the
formidable curse of a female disease. For not only did they
emasculate their bodies, but also they worked a further
degeneration in their souls, and, as far as in them lay,
were corrupting the whole of mankind.

Most of the prevalent myths and prejudices concerning
male homosexuality find expression here, such as the myth
of effeminacy—the idea that homosexuals must choose to
play the active-masculine role or the passive-feminine role,
that homosexuals recruit others, that there are specific
diseases associated with homosexuality. There is no concept
of a homosexual relationship based on the mutual love of
the persons. When we turn to the Fathers of the Christian
Church, there is no doubt whatever that they accepted
without question that the sin of the Sodomites was their
particular and inordinate addiction to homosexual practices,
particularly pederasty, and it was for this reason that God
punished them. In the Apostolic Constitutions we read: Thou
shalt not corrupt boys: for this wickedness is contrary to
nature and arose from Sodom." The Old Testament authors
and Jesus himself identified the primary sin of Sodom with
inhospitality to the stranger. We are dealing here with one of
the supremely ironic paradoxes of history. For two thousand
years in the Christian west, homosexuals have been the victims
of inhospitable treatment. Condemned by the Church, they
have been the victims of persecution, denial of civil rights,

torture and even death. In the name of a mistaken identity of the crime of Sodom and Gomorrah, the true crime has been —and continues to be—repeated ever after.

THE POSITIVE TREATMENT OF SAME SEX RELATIONS IN THE OLD TESTAMENT

Every text that refers to homosexual activity with a judgment of condemnation also refers to aggravating circumstances such as idolatry, sacred prostitution, promiscuity, violent rape, seduction of children and violation of guests' rights. Nowhere is there a specific text that rejects all homosexual activity as such independent of these circumstances. On the contrary, in a few instances where a loving homosexual relation is presented it is dealt with approval and respect. The most important example of this is the story of David and Jonathan in 1 Samuel.

In Chapter 18, we are told: "After David had finished talking to Saul, Jonathan's soul became closely bound to David's…. Jonathan made a pact with David to love him as his own soul; he took off the cloak he was wearing and gave it to David, and his armor too, even his sword, his bow and his belt." The Scripture goes on to report that Saul became jealous of David and attempted to kill him. Failing in that attempt, Saul plotted to have David killed in battle. Later in the story when Jonathan came out to visit David in hiding, we read: "The kissed each other and both shed many tears." My Hebrew scholar friends pointed out to me that the Hebrew text says "they released themselves" and could with equal validity be translated: "They ejaculated." The story ends with David's lament for Jonathan when he learns of his death:

> O Jonathan, in your death I am stricken,
> I am desolate for you, Jonathan my brother,
> Very dear to me you were,
> Your love to me more wonderful
> Than the love of a woman.

There is no condemnation connected to this beautiful statement of an intense interpersonal love relation.

The second example is taken from the book of Ruth, the story of Ruth and Naomi. When Naomi was forced to leave for a new home she urged her servant Ruth to leave her, but Ruth responded:

> Do not press me to leave you and to turn back from your company;
> For wherever you go, I shall go.
> Wherever you live, I will live.
> Your people shall be my people,
> And your God, my God.
> Wherever you die, I will die
> And there I will be buried.
> May Yahweh do this thing to me
> And more also,
> If ever death should come between us.

This pact of loving friendship between two women has become the primary biblical model for lesbian relations.

Play and The Song of Songs

The Song of Songs: The primary Revelation in the Old Testament of God's Intention for Human Sex as Play

No doubt the definitive revelation of how God intended human sexuality to be exercised in the Old Testament is to be found in the story of the two gardens. James Nelson points out in his book, *Between Two Gardens: Reflections on Sexuality and Religious Experience*, the period in which we live today falls between the time of the Garden of Eden depicted in Genesis 2 and the post-Redemption erotic garden depicted in the Song of Songs. A careful reading of Genesis 2 leaves no doubt that God intended all expressions of human sexuality to be expressions of human play. Play and sexual love have always been closely linked. The ancient Sanskrit term for coitus, *kridaratnam*, translates literally as "the jewel of all games."

In Genesis, before sin entered their world, humans are pictured as perfectly at home in that world and as completely accepting their bodies and the body's erotic dimension. There was no body-soul dualism. They had no trouble integrating sex into their loving companionship with each other in the presence of a loving God. But then sin entered their world. As a result of sin humans became ashamed of and alienated from their bodies. They objectified their own and others' bodies as sexual objects subject to lust and contempt. Sexual activity was transformed from a joy-filled play activity to a form of degradation. Our sex lives ceased to be play and became permeated with shame, contempt, insecurity and anxiety, and thus became more like work than play. As Nelson points out, the historical roots of sexual alienation are not difficult to find. They emerged as two intertwining dualisms. Spiritualistic dualism (spirit over body, mind over matter), championed by the Neo-Platonists, this dualism viewed the immortal spirit as a temporary prisoner in a mortal, corruptible body. The good life and, indeed, salvation requires escape from the flesh into spirit. Sexist or patriarchal dualism (man over woman), which is the twin of spiritualism, involves the systematic subordination of women in interpersonal relations, in institutions, in thought forms and in religious life. But the two dualisms became inextricably intertwined as men assumed to themselves superiority in spirit and reason while identifying women with body, earthiness, irrationality and instability.

As Sebastian Moore points out in his book *Jesus: Liberator of Desire*, Adam and Eve are portrayed in Genesis as being ashamed of their mortal bodies and their sexuality. They wanted to disembody themselves and become pure spirits like God. To rescue us from that sin of pride and redeem us, the Word became flesh and God gave us the gift of immortal bodies through resurrection with Christ rather than the human effort to become immortal souls by our own efforts and by disowning the body.

A central part of God's redemptive plan in Christ was to overcome all alienations and restore the integrity and playfulness of human sexuality. In his book, *Song of Love: A Biblical Understanding of Sex*, Helmut Gollwitzer points out that a redeemed, wholesome, and playful human sexuality is portrayed beautifully in the biblical text of the Song of Songs. Gollwitzer notes that the love extolled in this text is an illicit love. The lovers are not married and are of different races. (In fact, some scholars argue that there is some reason to suspect that the two lovers are two men in a gay relation. I will deal with this later.)

> Look, says the Bible, see these two lovers, how they delight in each other, each pleased with the body of the other. How excited they are as they gaze at the full length of the other's naked body. How they yearn for night to come so that they can embrace and be united. They are Adam and Eve in paradise, free of shame, in the happiness of sex. This is the way it was intended.... How could you possibly regard this as sinful? Why would you equate sexuality with immorality? Look at how all there senses

are brought into play—seeing, hearing, smelling, tasting, touching! This sensuality is the morality of their love because it is a love, as God wants it to be, a fully human love, planned for human beings.

There is nothing subhuman or animal about it, no relic of the earthly to be painfully endured, as if we have to strive to become purely spiritual beings. Nothing is so unlike the animal as human sexuality. It is not confined to periods of being in heat, nor does it merely serve the continuation of the species. It is not limited to the specific genital activity of procreation but encompasses the entire person in an act of complete concentration on and attention to the sex partner.

Gollwitzer points out that even if the Song of Songs extols an illicit form of love, outside an extrinsically imposed set of rules, it does not give us carte blanche to engage in a totally unstructured and uninhibited sexuality. There is a structure present in the sexuality of Song of Songs, but it is a structure that is no longer legalistic and repressive, but rather based in the nature of what it means to be human and compatible with the true freedom of the Gospels. That structure is identical with the conditions that make a human action play. At this point then, to understand ideal human sexual activity, we must undertake an analysis of work and play.

Human Sexuality as a Form of Play

The Conditions of Possibility for Human Work and Play

I n the Gospels, liberation is always a sign of the presence of the Holy Spirit, the Spirit of Love. Wherever and whenever true human liberation occurs, we can be certain of the presence and the activity of God's Spirit. Let us reflect on one type of human liberation implied in God's gift of his spirit of love—liberation from the "work ethic" so that a spirit of play may take its place.

The Work Ethic

One of the deepest values of American culture is the work ethic. The value judgment that accompanies this ethic is that our value as human beings lies in the work we do. We have to earn our value through our work. That work has frequently been understood in the past, in a very narrow sense, as the production of material goods. The logical conclusion of this kind of thinking is that our moral goodness depends on our willingness to commit ourselves to duty for its own sake in the form of difficult and dehumanizing work. Immanuel Kant, for example, was convinced that our worst distraction from moral duty was the search for pleasure and happiness.

The work ethic is so much a part of our culture and of ourselves that leisure time causes us very real difficulty. The average American feels very guilty when he or she is unemployed or on vacation. Perhaps for a few days they regard their leisure as valuable because it prepares them to return to work with renewed energy and enthusiasm. But any leisure beyond what is strictly necessary produces deep-seated feelings of uselessness, guilt and self-condemnation. A dramatic example is the common experience of retired persons who literally lose their will to live once their regular employment in the community is ended.

Perhaps the most dramatic expression of the work ethic in recent history was the directive sent by the Emperor Joseph of Belgium in the early 1900s to the administrators of the Belgium territory of the Congo. In this directive, he pointed out that the basis of all civilization was, in his opinion, the spirit of work. Consequently, if he were to fulfill his duty of civilizing the Congo, he must teach the natives the spirit of work. He, therefore, ordered that the natives be gathered together into work camps, where they would be assigned daily quotas of work, such as gathering so many pounds of latex or laying so many miles of railroad ties. If anyone failed to execute his or her daily quota, drastic penalties were to be applied, such as the amputation of a hand.

A stark contrast to the emperor's attitude may be seen in a Pygmy community from the rain forests of Africa who were featured in a recent television documentary. These people rose at dawn and did about an hour's work, such as gathering fruit, preparing meals and repairing the thatched roofs of their huts, which was all the work they had to do to obtain the necessities of life. All the rest of the day they played. They held ceremonial dances and set up contests to see who could swing the farthest on jungle vines. This people's philosophy of life, or rather their theology, involved the belief that they were children of a loving divine father who enjoyed their play. Thus their play was the most important element in their lives. Through joyous play they manifested their gratitude to God for their existence. If one of them was to become anxious and began to collect more bananas than he needed for the day and hoard things and have no time for play, his neighbors would think that he was sick or had lost his faith and trust in their god.

These were the people that the Emperor Joseph thought had to be taught the value of work. But the only way to do so was to destroy their theology, their belief that their God loved them for what they are and not for what they do. One would also have to destroy their psychological health, that is, their confidence in their self-worth. They would have to learn to be anxious about their value as people and feel that they must somehow prove themselves by what they can produce in the way of practical results through hard work to be worthy of God's love. Human work behavior is always based in anxiety, and all anxiety, as Bishop Fulton Sheen was fond of saying, is a form of atheism.

The work ethic reached its culmination in American culture where it fused with the frontier spirit, Native (or American) Pragmatism and American Puritanism. Certainly, this ethic served a purpose as long as the average life span was just above thirty-five and we were busy meeting the challenge of the frontier in our collective effort to build a great industrial nation. Today, however, the work ethic is running into a number of inherent contradictions. These contradictions, which will become progressively more manifest in time, are all connected with the cybernetic revolution. For the first time in its history, humanity has the means to turn over most of the real work of providing food, clothing and shelter to machines. The vast majority of new jobs today are in the field of human services. The contradiction lies in the fact that our psychology is still caught up in the work ethic, although the amount of work we do and the time devoted to it has been and in all likelihood will continue to be reduced dramatically. In my lifetime, the workweek has been reduced from a ten hour, six-day week to an eight hour, five-day week. Further reduction is resisted strenuously because of the work ethic. In many European nations the workweek has already been reduced to a ten-hour, four day week and vacation time has been increased to two months. We begin work much later in life. We retire much earlier. And we live much longer. As a result, the time we have for leisure and play has greatly increased.

Another contradiction in the work ethic is that it holds up affluence and leisure as goals in order to motivate people to work harder, when the very achievement of these goals leads to a sense of loss of personal value and the ostensible reward becomes more of a curse than a blessing. The practice of giving the retiring employee a gold watch at the time when he will least need it seems ironic indeed.

The greatest flaw in the work ethic is that it deprives us of the ability to live in the present moment and renders us victims of the tyranny of time. When one is working, the activity is not meaningful in itself but only in terms of what comes after... the money earned, the leisure or success or prestige gained. We endure the drudgery of the present in hope of what the future will bring.

One's whole life can be caught up in this attitude with the result that the quality of life is seriously diminished. The high-school student waits for graduation, the college student waits for graduate school, the graduate student waits for a job, the worker waits for a vacation, the vacationer waits to go back to work, and the veteran worker waits for retirement. Our whole life may be spent waiting for what comes next. Then death intervenes and in a way, it can be said that we never really existed, because we never found time to do something for its own sake, that is to say we never played.

THE CURSE OF WORK

The fundamental theological myth concerning work in Christian culture is found in Genesis, where the first humans are portrayed as living in the Garden of Eden, in paradise. There, like the pygmies in the rain forest, they played in the presence of God. But then they sinned, and the curse visited

on them because of that sin was the loss of an awareness
of God's loving presence. They became anxious and were
told: "with sweat on your brow shall you eat your bread."
(Gen.3:19). In other words, the need to work was a result of
their sin.

From this viewpoint the whole history of humanity to the
present day can be understood as a progressive effort, based
in the blood, sweat and tears of our ancestors, to liberate us
from the curse of work. Today, because of the cybernetic
revolution we stand on the threshold of that day of liberation.
In any case, work was originally understood as a curse based
on sin, but the work ethic distorts the curse into a blessing
and tries to keep humanity subject to that curse in an age
where liberation has become a distinct possibility.

Another essential aspect of the work ethic is that it
leads to the subordination of persons to things. The work
ethic demands that we judge our value on the basis of our
productivity. Our relations with persons are considered
secondary and largely irrelevant. Recent political proposals
to reform welfare are frequently based on a dramatic appeal
to the American work ethic. The welfare system is being
reformed by forcing massive numbers of people back into
the job market.

The interesting aspect of the proposed reform is that
the mother on welfare, who stays at home and dedicates
herself entirely to raising her children, to developing their
personalities and serving their needs, is not considered to be
making a worthwhile contribution to the community. The
proposal that was voted in by a large majority in Congress
was that welfare mothers be forced to leave their home in

order to work and their children be placed in day care. This same kind of prejudice in the past is evident in the inferior salaries paid to teachers, nurses, social workers, anyone who provides human services but do not work with things.

This subordination of persons to things is built into the very fabric of our society; we often hear of one or another American industry demanding the same sort of loyalty from its employees that one would expect from a member of the family. Yet once the individual can no longer make profitable contribution, industry no longer feels any reciprocal loyalty. In recent years, especially, many people have been laid off just one year before they were eligible for retirement. And Chairmen of the Board have been amply rewarded with bonuses for their ruthlessness in such behavior. The only family many businesses resemble is the Eskimo family of old, where the day grandmother's teeth gave out and she could no longer chew the sealskins, she was put out on an ice shelf and bid a tearful goodbye.

It is instructive to recall the book which was one time the bible of the aspiring young American businessman, Dale Carnegie's *How to Win Friends and Influence People*. This book, in my mind, should rate as the most immoral book ever written. What I understand to be its message is that one should pretend genuine interest in other persons, not for their own sake, but in order to use them. This is precisely the meaning of the word hypocrisy. One practices smiling, saying the right thing and pretending to have the same interests in order to win the other's confidence and make a sale. One's object is to selfishly get ahead in life even by deception where necessary. This book was written totally within the context of the work ethic.

Gay and lesbian people are particularly susceptible to becoming victims of the work ethic. Having been taught from childhood that their difference is somehow bad and makes them unworthy of love and acceptance, gay people frequently feel that they must outperform all their peers in order to compensate. Workaholism based on anxiety has been a common disease in the lesbian and gay community.

WHAT MAKES HUMAN ACTIVITY PLAY?

WHAT IS PLAY?

What, then, is the alternative to the work ethic? The opposite of work is not sloth or inactivity; rather, it is play. Play should be understood as a basic form of human activity, irreducible to anything else.

Most analysts of play make the mistake of reducing it to a means to something else, and that 'something else' is usually work. This is the case with the type of psychological study that attempts to explain children's play behavior as an instinctual process whereby they learn to cope with reality, a preparatory behavior to work wherein one develops new skills. Play certainly achieves this, but if this were the child's conscious intention, that activity would no longer be play.

Because play occupies such an important position in our lives, we would do well to focus our efforts on cultivating the possibility of play within the human community. The first condition necessary for a human activity to be play is that the human activity must be meaningful in itself and not be related to a goal that lies beyond the playful action itself; it must be totally meaningful here and now. A perfect illustration of this quality is the activity of dancing.

This aspect of play also has a close connection with the quality of our interpersonal relationships. If it is impossible for us to live fully in the present moment, then we will never be able to be present fully for anther person. The ability to do so and, consequently, the ability to be fully present for another is probably the primary reason why, when we succeed in playing, we experience such intense joy and fulfillment. Anyone who has met an extraordinary spiritual or saintly person immediately is struck by their ability to be totally present in the here and now to the one they are encountering.

As the German poet Schiller put it, "Humans are only fully human when they play." Johan Huizinga, in his classic book *Homo Ludens: A Study of the Play Element in Culture*, sees play as the fullest expression of our humanity because it is the fullest expression of human freedom. Play is always an expression of personal initiative and of the self, free from all extrinsic constraint. Huizinga builds a good case for the thesis that all human civilization—commerce, science, law and all the arts—has its foundation not in work but in play. Even religious worship at its best should be a form of play. The purpose of all liturgies is "to teach us how to celebrate our existence." Huizinga points out that if play is the foundation of all civilization, to lose the sense of play is to threaten that very foundation.

The gay community has always been a community with an extraordinary freedom to play. Society is keenly aware that creative gay people are represented in the arts—the theater, the plastic arts, music, ballet, film, fashion, out of all proportion to their numbers in the population at large. The incredible loss to the entire human community of creative talent because of the AIDS-related deaths of so many gifted men is painful proof of this thesis.

Some of that freedom to play comes, I believe, from the gay community's acceptance of its exiled status. Gays are frequently no longer involved in competing. As a result they are much freer to develop an aesthetic sense and to engage in activities for their own sake. Jung attributes the creativity of the gay community to its ability to be in touch with the feminine as well as the masculine aspects of the self.

In order to clarify further what I mean by play, I must make an important distinction. The very same activity may be work or play. Whether or not one is working or playing depends not so much on what one is doing but on the spirit and the conditions under which one does it. The person who is gardening on a weekend may be doing back-breaking work, but still is playing.

This leads us to the next condition necessary for an activity to take the form of play. Play always calls into question the type of interpersonal relation within which the activity takes place. An example would be the relation of two people on the job and the relationship of the same two people on the company bowling team. People involved in the game are playing and enjoying themselves. In a game such as bowling it is interesting to note how giving a handicap can change the nature of the bowlers' attitude. The purpose of the handicap is to allow even the least skilled player to compete on an equal basis with his or her teammates. In this way the least skilled person achieves a sense of equality and his or her anxiety over success or failure is lessened.

Another key difference between work and play is that the attitude of work is always based on anxiety. Frequently, people in industry strive to increase production by increasing anxiety concerning job security or pay raises. Play, in contrast, can only take place where there is a felt sense of security. Animals, for example, will engage in playful behavior, but only if they are well fed and feel safe from their enemies. Psychologists have observed that a seriously disturbed child will cease to play. The only way that disturbed child can be freed to play once again is to give him or her the felt security of being loved. The unconditional love of the mother frees the infant to play. Conditioned love results in pathology, i.e. to the feeling that one must earn love through work.

Some theologians have argued that adults are free to play only when they become aware that God loves them for their own sake and not for what they do. "What proves that God loves us is that Christ died for us while we were still sinners." (Rom. 5:8). Thus the ability to be free to play all of life in the presence of a loving God is a central message of revelation. God, our parent in heaven, through the redemption wrought by Jesus Christ, has freed us from the curse of work and created for us once again the freedom to play.

Conditions of Possibility Of Play

Thus the first and most important condition of possibility for play has to do with the type of community within which the activity takes place. There are two basic types of human community: the functional and the personal. In a functional community, the interrelations between persons are not meaningful in themselves but only as a means of productivity of some sort. Authority in a functional community exists in order to coordinate the efforts of the group toward that productivity.

A personal community, such as the family, is quite different. The community is its own end; it is the loving interrelationships between the members that justify the existence of the community. Productivity within the personal community is secondary and has its source in the overflow of the joy and love that unites the members of the community. Authority in a personal community has its primary task to promote dialogue, to bring about personal interaction and mutual affirmation among the members. The personal community is based on the fact that we need each other. We need others to affirm us in our existence, to make us feel that we mean something and that we have value. We need the security of being loved and giving love in return. It is only to the degree that we find ourselves members of a true personal community that we have the necessary security and confidence to be able to play.

The ultimate source of the freedom to play is God's unconditional love for us, a love that we cannot merit and we do not have to earn. As the good news of God's love penetrates our hearts, we are freed to be able to love each other unconditionally. It is love that creates the space in which we are free to dance and sing. It is love that frees us to be able to play. Our only appropriate response to this gift of unconditional love and the freedom to play is gratitude.

I will finish this reflection on human play with an anecdote from J.D. Salinger's *Raise High the Roof Beam, Carpenters*. Salinger reports a conversation between the young hero of the novel and his older brother, who has just become champion marble player of all Brooklyn. The younger brother asks: "Seymour, what is the secret of your success?" Seymour ponders awhile and answers: "Don't Aim!" I believe the whole secret of life lies in those two words.

SEX AS PLAY

The structure that Gollwitzer points out is present in the sexual activity in *The Song of Songs* is identical with the conditions necessary for human play. First of all, play activity must be meaningful in itself and not be related to a result that lies beyond the playful action. Healthy, playful human sex requires that the sex partners treat each other as ends in themselves; a failure to do so reduces one's partner to a sexual object. To deal with any human as a means rather than an end in him or herself is to degrade and demean that person. The essential immorality of prostitution is not that it involves sex outside of marriage, but that it involves one person using another as an object and that object allowing him or herself to be used.

This is also the essential flaw in the traditional work-related sexual ethics based on procreation. Any sexual act undertaken exclusively for the purpose of procreation both destroys the play value of sex and reduces the partners to workers interested solely in seeking a future product from a present action. It is interesting to note that there is no mention of procreation anywhere in the Song of Songs or in Chapter 2 of Genesis.

As we have seen, the conditions necessary for play to take place are identical with the conditions necessary for love to exist between two persons. The most important of these is that the partners see each other as equals. Whenever patriarchal dualism flourishes and the man sees himself as essentially superior to the woman, a necessary condition for true love and playfulness in the sexual encounter is absent. This inequality of the partners in heterosexist relations is a major cause of the breakdown of the family. I believe that this is a key reason why God's Spirit is leading us into the liberation issue of gay marriage. Gay marriage is usually totally based on the equality of the partners and thus serves as an ideal model for the renewal of heterosexual relations on a healthier basis.

In the Song of Songs, the woman's equal status with the male is striking. It is not an accident that the book begins with the woman's passionate words: "Your lips cover me with kisses; your love is better than wine." (1:2) This equality between the partners keeps them from ever pressuring or manipulating each other. Each invites the other to a sexual encounter but profoundly respects the other's freedom. As Gollwitzer puts it: "The other is always wanted as a person, a partner; not as a thing, a means of sexual gratification. No one is reduced to a mere sexual object. All expressions of affection are appeals to the free emotions of the beloved, voicing the hope that the other will respond with the same love."

Recent psychodynamic theory recognizes that the basic drive of the human psyche in not toward pleasure (as Freud believed) but toward intimacy. The human yearns to move out of isolation into the deepest possible union with fellow humans and ultimately with God. Consequently, the sex-drive is the physical dimension of a human need to escape isolation and alienation for a profound physical and spiritual union. The search for sexual fulfillment is thus one manifestation of a search for union with God. And achieving that intimacy results in intense pleasure, both physical and spiritual. In fact, the Song of Songs makes the claim that in sexual climax there can be an experience of God him/herself. "The flash of it is a flash of fire, it is the breath of Yahweh himself."

I remember an event that took place nearly 65 years ago on my first day in high school. I was a scared, lonely thirteen year old, starved for affection. One day I was placing my books in my locker in the basement when suddenly someone, I never knew who, came around the corner and caught me up from behind in a hearty bear hug for a fleeting moment and then disappeared. I shall never forget the profound pleasure I felt in that affectionate and erotic hug. I think I spent the rest of that year putting books in my locker and taking them out again hoping for the return of the mysterious hugger, but to no avail.

Love for the Unique Individual

There is yet another condition that must be met for a sexual encounter to be playful, namely that one's partner is loved as a unique individual. The bull does not care which cow it mates with, any cow will do. But humans do care about the uniqueness of their sexual partner. One's partner is not simply a representative of the opposite sex or the same sex, interchangeable with any other, a mere sex object. Rather, one's partner is a unique and irreplaceable "thou," one particular person whose place no other can take, this man, this woman, this person alone is loved.

This attitude contrasts sharply with the "Playboy" view of sex. Those who subscribe to this view feel free to use— and even abuse—their partner selfishly, without scarcely any sense of responsibility and concern. The perfect Playboy cartoon shows a man and woman naked in bed together with the man asking the woman, "Why talk about love at a time like this?" This attitude is perfectly symbolized by the Playboy bunny costume, which, with its tail and ears, is an ideal way to dehumanize and depersonalize one's sexual object. Don't forget that the sexual idol the Israelites worshipped took the form of a golden calf.

Intimacy, both physical and spiritual, is precisely the goal of playful sex. But, as we have seen, in order to have the freedom to play and to overcome self-consciousness, we must have the felt security of being loved. The primary purpose of a relationship of love is to enable the partners to affirm each other continuously through shared activities in an atmosphere of security and trust. Love gives us that freedom.

Those who hold the old-fashioned dualistic view of love tend to posit a sharp division between spiritual love, which is directed toward the person, and the purely physical gratification of the sex drive. In reality, there are not two different kinds of love—all genuine love has its physical aspects. There are, however, two kinds of sex—alpha sex and omega sex—that need to be distinguished. Alpha sex involves using one's partner selfishly to obtain one's own sexual gratification. This kind of sexual activity seldom results in true intimacy and provides no escape from loneliness. On the contrary, it intensifies loneliness. Clients have told me many times that their sense of painful isolation only increased after an all night orgy in a bathhouse.

Omega sex, on the other hand, occurs when there is a complete fusion of sensual and personal love. Each partner is a source of pleasure for the other and each can experience pleasure only by being a source of pleasure for the other. As Gollwitzer puts it: "Self centeredness—I need this person for myself, for my own happiness—is the power of Eros, whereas the knowledge that I will be happy only through the happiness of my partner is the wisdom of Eros. Eros understands that we get what we want, not only when and if the partner's needs are also met, but precisely in and through their being met."

As a psychotherapist, I am intensely aware that I am dealing here with an ideal goal of human sexual growth and maturity. As Nelson notes, most of us find ourselves at some place between the two gardens, aspiring to omega sex but practicing alpha sex, but hopefully growing daily in our ability to integrate our sexual activity into our capacity to love.

I am also aware that many people are psychically so injured that they are incapable of a full human relationship of intimacy and love. Yet these persons have a right to some playful expression of their sexuality and their search for intimacy. I agree with Norman Pittenger that there are only three kinds of sexual activity between consenting adults: good, better and best sex. Apart from rape or child abuse, contrary to traditional Church teaching, it is difficult to sin seriously in a sexual gesture. I am reminded of a joke I heard years ago that contained a certain wisdom. A derelict went into a bar on the Bowery with a parakeet on his shoulder. He said to all the drinkers at the bar: "I'll go to bed with anyone who guesses the weight of my parakeet!" One man lifted his head from the bar and said: "Two hundred pounds!." "Close enough!" the derelict answered. The humor of the joke is that it speaks to every one of us in our loneliness. Two lonely people, both too wounded at this point in their life to form an intimate relationship, will know a moment of affection and a sharing of sexual pleasure, and this is good.

Gay Sexual Liberation

Like the love of the man and woman in the Song of Songs, all gay sexual love has been illicit, condemned by the law of society and the Church. Because of this, lesbian and gay sexual love has no models or rules to go by. After the Stonewall gay liberation revolution, the gay community undertook an all-out celebration of gay sexuality and a constant exploration of new forms of sexual fulfillment. Since any and all forms of gay sex, even that within a committed monogamous relationship, were considered by heterosexist society to be illegal and immoral by their very nature, the gay community was not prepared to recognize any moral or legal restraint on sexual behavior.

Many gays have realized that totally promiscuous sex deprives them of the deep intimacy that is the primary fruit of committed sexual relationships. As a result, in recent years the gay community is seeking recognition from both State and Church of their relationships as a legitimate form of human love worthy of being recognized as a marriage.

The church's attack on gay marriage as a threat to the family amazes me. As long as one's gay orientation had to be hidden, many gay men sought to hide their orientation by getting married. The majority of church divorces were based on the gayness of one or the other partner. Gay liberation and the possibility of gay marriage would free thousands of gay men to enter into a gay relation and no longer have to hide their orientation in a false heterosexual marriage. This would strengthen heterosexual marriage and the health and well-being of the entire human community.

In my thirty years of practice I am aware that thousands of gay and lesbian people were the ones who took care of their parents in their old age. Most families were blessed who had a gay son or lesbian daughter. How can the achievement of intimate committed relations be a threat to the family? On the contrary, as I will develop later on, gay marriage may be a resource for a renewal and strengthening of heterosexual relationships.

SEXUAL LIBERATION AND THE AIDS CRISIS

The first reaction of the gay community to AIDS during the late 80s and early 90s was a serious reevaluation of efforts toward sexual liberation, the "anything goes" attitude. There is a welcome and new emphasis on prudence and health consciousness in all sexual expression. There is also a new exploration of the kind of committed relationship that is appropriate to lesbian women and gay men and is not just a repetition of heterosexual models. The majority of lesbians and gay men today as they grow out of adolescence are consciously seeking a lover and the type of committed relationship that makes a love relationship possible.

A danger in the present situation is that many in the gay community could lose the freshness and the joy of their celebration of God's good gift of sexuality and regress into feelings of shame, guilt, and self-loathing for any expression of their sexuality. And, of course, the conservative homophobic Churches are doing their best to produce this regression among their followers. The possibility of having caring and playful sex still exists if both partners follow the guidelines for safe sex.

As I mentioned in my book *The Church and the Homosexual*, a paradoxical result of the AIDS crisis is that it is bringing gay love out of the closet! Before AIDS, the most visible members of the gay community were those who frequented the gay discos, bars and baths. These were the people associated with the so-called gay life-style. Those who were involved in committed, loving relationships for the most part remained closeted in order to protect each other's jobs, homes and families from the usually dire consequences of public exposure. AIDS has forced many couples to be public about their relationships as they cared for each other in the relatively public space of hospitals. I personally know many priests, ministers and family members who have been astonished by the depth of the love, mutual support, and self-sacrifices that characterize the relationships of many gay couples. This revelation laid the foundation of the present political effort to achieve the legal right for gay marriage.

THE MESSAGE OF THE SONG OF SONGS

Every element of the moral, sexual lovemaking portrayed in the Song of Songs can be, and frequently is, present in the sexual relationship of two gay men or two lesbian women who love each other. Consequently, there is no valid reason why their sexual unions should not be accepted, respected and valued by the church and by society.

Near the end of the Song of Songs we read:

> Set me like a seal on your heart,
> Like a seal on your arm.
> For love is as strong as Death,
> Jealously relentless as Sheol.
> The flash of it is a flash of fire
> A flame of Yahweh himself,
> Love no flood can quench,
> No torrent drown.
> Were a man to offer all the wealth of his house to
>   buy love,
> Contempt is all he would purchase. (8:6-7)

I remember as a youth in Buffalo, New York, a popular saying was that "Sexual love is God's gift to the poor." The authors of The Song of Songs believed that a loving experience of sexual pleasure could carry with it an experience of divine presence. This is a restatement of the biblical message that "God is love and if anyone loves they know God!"

A POSSIBLE SAME SEX INTERPRETATION OF THE LOVERS IN THE SONG OF SONGS

In his book *Ancient Answers to Modern Gay Problems*, Paul R. Johnson gives a plausible interpretation of the Song of Songs as a poem celebrating the love of two men for each other. Johnson explains that early Hebrew texts completely lacked written vowel sounds or "vowel points." The Song of Songs was originally written in consonantorial text, that is, words were spelled with only consonants—no vowels. Although the gender of the principal character in the Song is clearly male eighty-five percent of the time, there is a ten percent ambiguity. When the Mascretic scholars set about inscribing the ancient text (already seventeen centuries old) with vowel sounds in the 8th century AD, they, because of their own cultural prejudices, chose to feminize certain terms by inserting vowel points above, below, or in the consonants which would effectively change the meaning.

Johnson quotes one verse that he thinks is a definitive proof that the text is dealing with male lovers (7:10):

Because of your manliness
Your mouth surrenders to my male love
Direct and gentle into slumbering lips.

Johnson points out all the anomalies that follow from trying to interpret one of the lovers as female:

> If this person were female, she would be, according to the original text the most liberated women in all the world… She was not interested in marriage; she was not concerned with conception; she made many trips through the city streets at night searching for her beloved; she slept with the shepherds in their tent; she was a mountain climber; drove a chariot; was a much feared fighter; stalked wild animals; took the lead in the sex act; was a shield bearer; owned personal property, was a great fighter and wrestler; had a large nose, strong neck, and very tiny breasts. This beautiful ten percent woman possessed a huge body, wore a beard and was called a prince.

The time has come for a hermeneutic of suspicion to reclaim this song as originally a gay love song.

SEX IN THE NEW TESTAMENT

"This is my Body!" Let us hear anew those startling words. Let us see and hear Jesus speaking them over the bread at the Last Supper: Jesus desiring and willing to be with us in and through his human body until the end of time. If Jesus accepted classical dualism he should have been content to be with us though the gift of his spirit. But Jesus, because of his human love for us, wanted a bodily contact with every human that he loved. Jesus established the new covenant in his body and blood so that for all time the meeting place between God and humanity, the means of communication by which we become one with God and God becomes one with us, will be the flesh and blood of Jesus. Jesus chose to be one in the flesh with every human from now until the end of time. Let us reflect, then on the mystery of the human body, both Christ's body and our own.

When, as a young man, I made my first trip to Chicago, I remembered being very impressed by a statue by Rodin entitled *The Isolation of the Human Spirit*. The statue was hewn from a huge block of granite. Emerging from the stone, but still partially trapped in it, were the alternate bodies of men and women. Each figure was straining every muscle trying to reach around to the figures on either side of it, but none could touch more than the fingertips of the others.

Rodin's statue dramatically expresses the paradox of the human body. It is our body that keeps us apart from each other, allows us to be separate, unique individuals, autonomous and free. Yet the same body is the means by which we communicate and achieve union with the other.

Frequently, we Christians fail to accept our bodies as God intends us to accept them. And failing to accept our own bodies, we frequently fail to accept Christ's incarnation and the reality of his and our bodily resurrection. Sometimes we fall victims to those ancient heresies that, like Manicheans, see the body with its sexual drive and hungers as evil and a source of sin. We then are tempted to see ourselves as essentially a soul or spirit housed in a body, which we use but with which we are not identified. The corollary of this alienation from our God-given body is the view that human sexuality is something evil, something that can drive us away from God. Death then appears as a welcome release from the prison of the body, and we begin to understand the hereafter in terms of immortality of the soul instead of resurrection of the body.

But all this is not the teaching of Christ. On the contrary, it was Plato and the Greek pagan philosophers who taught the immortality of the soul or mind. They would judge the Christian message of resurrection of the body as pure foolishness. Jesus revealed an immortality that is to be achieved by a miraculous resurrection and transformation of the body.

One of the primary reasons for our denial of our bodies is the difficulty we experience with our sexual drive. As we evolve toward spiritual maturity, each of us must struggle with our sexual drive so that, with God's grace, it will cease to be a totally selfish destructive force and become instead a power integrated into our personality as a means of communicating love.

We have succeeded in integrating other bodily functions into our personality, such as eating, to the point where heaven itself is symbolized as a banquet and the family dinner has been fully integrated into our social and spiritual life. Just as there are prayers before and after a meal, so too there should be prayers before and after sex. To the extent that this idea shocks us, we may gauge the extent to which we remain alienated from our body and its God-given sexuality.

Every effort we make at communication—a handshake, for example, or a kiss, using our lips and mouth, not for eating as nature intended, but to produce speech—has a bodily non-genital sexual component. We are not spirits that use a body; we are our bodies. By the same token, sex is not just something we do; it is an inalienable dimension of what we are.

Let us look at the relation between love of God and love of our whole selves, including our body. There is a connection between fear of God and fear of the erotic dimension of our body.

By stating that there is really only one commandment, namely, the commandment to love, Jesus emphasized the special quality of our relationship to God in the new covenant. No longer are we to worship God in a spirit of fear, rather we are to relate to God as adopted children to a loving parent and not as slaves to a master. We must beware, then, of the kind of fear that can crush out the love of God from our hearts and lead us back into a worship of fear, a sort of post-Christian paganism.

You were not called to a spirit of slavery, to let fear into your life again. You were called to a spirit of adoption. You have the right to call your God *Abba*, that is, father.

Notice that in the first commandment Jesus orders us to love God with all our hearts. In the New Testament the heart is a symbol for the body and its feelings. We are exhorted to let the love of God penetrate our whole being, including the body and all its feelings. This affirms that there is a sensuous and even erotic dimension to our love of God, a dimension so essential to our ability to love as embodied human beings that to deny it would cripple our spiritual life as well.

I am reminded of a sermon Augustine once gave to the first community of celibate women in Hippo. Commenting on the biblical parable of the wise and foolish virgins, Augustine made the point that chastity in itself does not get anyone into heaven. Both the wise and foolish virgins were chaste, but only the wise virgins who had "oil in their lamps" were allowed into the wedding feast when the bridegroom arrived. What, Augustine asked, does oil in their lamps signify? His answer was that the oil in the lamps of the wise virgins signified their ability to express warm human love; whereas the foolish virgins were cold and distant, expecting to get into heaven because of their moralistic perfectionism. Augustine was making the point that there is a pathological as well as a healthy form of chastity. But in the end there is only one way to gain admittance to the heavenly banquet, and that is through the exercise of a warm human love.

Listen to the sensuality of this prayer of Saint Augustine:

> Late have I loved you, O Beauty, ever ancient, ever new. Late have I loved you!
>
> You were within me, but I was outside, and it was there that I searched for you. In my unloveliness I plunged into the lovely things which you created. You were with me, but I was not with you. Created things kept me from you, but if they had not been in you they would not have been at all.
>
> You called, you shouted, and you broke through my deafness. You flashed, you shone, and you dispelled my blindness. You breathed your fragrance on me, I drew in breath and now I pant for you. I tasted you, now I hunger and thirst for more. You touched me, and now I long for your peace.

Jesus tells us that the second part of his commandment is identical (*homoia*) to the first, that is, the commandment to love God is the same as the commandment to love our neighbor as our self. That identity is so strong that John feels free to say that if anyone claims to love God and nevertheless hates his neighbor, that person is a liar (1 John 4:20).

For most of us, love of God remains an abstraction, an idea to which nothing real corresponds, unless that love can be incarnated into our lives. Just as Jesus is the incarnation of God's love for us, so too most of us come through to a belief and trust in God's love through our experience of human love—the love of a parent, friend, partner or through a loving community. God loves us through our friends and lovers. Again to quote Saint Augustine: "Show me a human in love, and I will show you a human on the way to God."

Let us focus for a moment on the third dimension of Jesus' commandment: Love of self. Jesus tells us that we should love our neighbor as ourselves. A certain healthy narcissism is implied here. Love begins with oneself. Many have misinterpreted this commandment as love your neighbor more than yourself! Some even seem to think it means that you shall love your neighbor and hate yourself. These people replace a healthy narcissism with masochism and believe they are glorifying God through self-rejection and self-hatred. We can extend John's statement and add that those who claim they love their neighbor and hate themselves are unconscious liars. Anyone who interiorized *feminaphobia* and/or homophobia would be in that category.

The first and greatest commandment presupposes that all three loves—love of self, neighbor and God—are all of a piece. If one is missing, then the others cannot exist. Which brings us back to our bodies once again. I believe that the most profound and most frequent sin concerning our bodies and their erotic dimension has nothing to do with sexual activity. On the contrary, it has to do with the alienation from our body and its sexual feelings and our effort to reject or repress the erotic dimension of our being, an effort that represents a refusal of God's good gift of sexuality and a distrust of creation.

All alienation from God's good creation is the result of sin, and alienation from our bodies is depicted in Scripture as the root of sin. We read in Genesis that the first humans, Adam and Eve, felt perfectly at home with themselves, their bodies and with God until they sinned. It was only then they became alienated from and ashamed of their nakedness. As a consequence of that alienation from their bodies, they also became alienated from each other and from God. Love of neighbor disappeared and Cain even went so far as to slay his brother Abel. Humanity had lost the reality of the loving presence of God.

In a work entitled *The Feast of Love*, Pope John Paul II, writing from a heterosexist dualistic and patriarchal perspective, sees the sin of Adam and Eve as "lustful activity." After the harmony between God and humanity had been broken, the lower, i.e. the sexual, nature of human beings no longer obeyed the higher. Sebastian Moore, in a masterful critique of this book, points out that three different times the author of Genesis identifies Adam's and Eve's sin not as lustful activity, but rather as a willful alienation from their body and its sexual feelings. They wanted to become pure body-less spirit just as God is by their own efforts

For Adam and Eve, the body became an object over against the self, the source of their mortality and something to be constrained out of fear or to be indulged as a dehumanized source of pleasure. Either way, the alienated body is divorced from the spiritual self. Both these extremes miss the point that God intended sexual wholeness to be a part of our redemption.

If every human being experiences a certain degree of alienation from her or his body and its sexual feelings, how much more alienated can lesbians and gay men become if they accept the Church teaching that their orientation is an "objective disorder," a tendency to evil, and a defect in creation. And how much more difficult is the struggle gay people must undergo to accept themselves and their sexuality with gratitude to God.

In my work as a psychotherapist over many years to the lesbian, gay, bisexual and transgendered community, I became aware how many people, in an effort to repress their gay sexual feelings, crushed out all feelings whatsoever and lived lives devoid of warmth and intimacy. There is also a connection between alienation from the body and the depersonalization of sex. The unloving suppression of the self's erotic needs frequently leads to a destructive acting out of those needs. This, in my opinion, is the primary mechanism operative in the clergy pedophilia crisis. What we reject in ourselves, we tend to project outward: sexism, heterosexism, homophobia, hatred of women or hatred of men, racism, sexual abuse of children, etc.

It has always been the prophetic role of lesbians and gay men to lead the Church and Western culture toward embracing embodiment, a sense of identity with the body and its sensuousness. We must let our "word become flesh!" This has, as always, been the special message entrusted by

God to the lesbian and gay community. We must give up our dualistic, escapist concept of being immortal souls encased in a mortal body that we must use but not identify with. We must learn how to live in, enjoy and celebrate our bodies and their sexuality with gratitude to God.

Four Affirmations Of The Body

Paradoxically, Christianity, which historically has been so antisexual in practice, differs from the other world religions in having such a positive attitude toward the human body. Christian revelation contains at least four essential affirmations of the body, including its sexual dimension.

The first is the biblical account of creation, which is the original creation narrative, predating the first chapter by over 500 years. God announces: "It is not good that man should be alone. I will make him a helpmate" (2:18). The first human couple was thus united by a sexual bond. The same theme is taken up in the Song of Songs, an entire book of the bible given over to a grateful celebration of God's gift of erotic love.

The second affirmation of the body is the Incarnation. As the Gospel of John tells us, "the Word was made flesh and lived among us" (John 1:14). Jesus was a sexual being; he underwent circumcision. If Jesus accepted and rejoiced in an embodied sexual existence, then we too should let our word become flesh, we should be able to accept and rejoice in our sexual body.

The third affirmation is the establishment of the Eucharist as Jesus' memorial: "This is my body!" Christ could have chosen to be with us for all time through his spirit alone, but the human Jesus chose to be with us in and through his human body as well. He wanted to stay "in touch."

The fourth is the Resurrection. We do not share the pagan concept of eternal life as a life only of the spirit, with the body serving merely as a temporary shell to be discarded. In some transformed way, our body will be part of our identity for all eternity.

We can get to heaven only in and through our sexual, mortal body. Therefore, we must do battle with and overcome our alienation from our body and its sexuality. This is another dimension of our salvation and one of the healing graces Jesus won for us. Adam and Eve, by wanting to become like God, grew ashamed of their sexual bodies. Jesus, on the other hand, who was the "Word of God," chose to become flesh. And because the Word became flesh, we can allow our word to become flesh; we can overcome all alienation from our body and accept our identity with it. We must trust that the Creator so designed the self's erotic nature that it is intrinsically aimed, not at an impersonal sexual hedonism, but at personal sexual communion.

Thus our task is, with the help of God's grace, to integrate that sexual nature into the power to love—to love ourselves, to love each other and ultimately to love God with our whole being. Even our compulsive, promiscuous sexuality is a flawed search for unity with each other and with God. A word of peace, encouragement and hope to all those who are finding this struggle difficult: the outcome is guaranteed, the grace of God is there, and the day will come when the struggle is over.

Jesus' great high-priestly prayer for us at the Last Supper was a prayer for our unity:

> *I pray not only for these,*
> *But for those also*
> *Who through their words will believe in me.*
> *May they all be one.*
> *Father, may they be one in us,*
> *As you are in me and I am in you,*
> *So that the world may believe it was you that sent me.*
> *I have given them the glory you gave to me,*
> *That they may be one as we are one.*
> *With me in them and you in me,*
> *May they be so completely one*
> *That the world will realize that it was you who sent me*
> *And that I have loved them as much as you loved me.*
>
> *(John. 17:20-23)*

The whole meaning and direction of our spiritual growth is a movement from isolation and alienation into greater unity with each other. At Holy Communion each of us receives the body of Christ and being one with the body of Christ we become one with each other. This is a symbolic prophesy of the mysterious and joyful transformation of our bodies at the Resurrection, when our bodies will become the perfect means of communication and oneness.

In his book on sexual theology, James Nelson tells us:

That which is greater than you accepts your body, which you often reject.

Your sexual feelings and unfulfilled yearnings are accepted.

You are accepted in your ascetic attempts at self justification or in your hedonistic alienation from the true meaning of your sexuality.

You are accepted in those moments of sexual fantasy which come unbidden and which delight and disturb you.

You are accepted in your femininity and in your masculinity and you have elements of both.

Simply accept the fact that you are accepted as a sexual person.

If that happens to you, you experienced grace.

WHAT WENT WRONG?

THE LOSS OF THE SACRAMENTAL SENSE

I n the National Catholic Reporter (Oct. 3, 2003) Eugene Cullen Kennedy wrote a remarkable article on the loss of a sacramental sense among the leaders in the Roman Catholic Church. The article was entitled "Healing the Wound: The Sacraments and Human Sexuality." Kennedy claims that the pedophilia crisis in the Church is only the tip of the iceberg of a much more fundamental crisis.

The foundational crisis is the impairment or complete loss by church leaders of the sacramental sense, that feeling for the theological principal of sacramentality, the notion that all reality, both animate and inanimate, is potentially or in fact the bearer of God's presence and the instrument of God's saving activity on humanity's behalf.

Forfeiting this sacramental sense in order to maintain hierarchical control, they shattered the wholeness of creation in general and of the human person in particular. This wrenches sexuality out of human personality as brutally as an Aztec priest's cutting out the heart of a young girl, both sacrifices of wholeness to the blood appetite of meagerly imagined gods. This gutting of human personality destroys its sacramental integrity, bringing a darkness at noon, the murky light in which the sacramental is devoured by the literal... While men and women search for these lost symbols of healthy life, the subtleties and the subtext of beaten down sexuality manifest themselves both in the abuse of the Body of Christ that marks the fundamental sacramental crisis and in the abuse of children's bodies that grew, slowly and surely and largely in the dark, out of it. Make healthy sexuality falsely evil and you make clear the way for the true evil of unhealthy sexuality.

Kennedy traces this loss of a sacramental sense back to Augustine. It can be said that Augustine did not so much convert to Christianity as he did infect the early Christian Church with his Manichean distrust of the body and its sexuality. In fact, he taught that God did not originally intend human beings to be sexual and that all sexual arousal, passion and pleasure was a result of original sin. One of the great ironies of Christian history is that what was originally portrayed in Genesis as the sin of Adam and Eve, to become alienated and ashamed of their bodies and desirous to become pure spirits, under Augustine influence became the official policy of the early Christian Church and the healthy holistic understanding that Jesus had of human sexuality was lost for centuries.

This acceptance of dualism, and the understanding that everything sexual was tinged by sin, led to a progressive loss of a holistic understanding of Jesus. Since Jesus could not be touched by sin, the Church was uncomfortable with the human sexual side of Jesus and progressively dehumanized him into pure spirit. In fact, the Jesuit introduction of devotion to the Sacred Heart of Jesus in the 18th century was an effort to restore full humanity to our understanding of the dehumanized Jesus of the Middle Ages who was so spiritualized that he disappeared into thin air.

It was this same misunderstanding and discomfort with the body and its sexuality that led to the imposition of celibacy on the clergy and the persecution of married clergy and their wives. A constant demand put on celibate clergy to repress and deny their human need for sexual intimacy and no recognition for their need for a healthy psycho-sexual development set the scene for the pedophile crisis.

The sacraments are addressed to us as whole human persons in ways as fundamentally and utterly earthly and human as we are, given not as antidotes for being human but to nourish us, just as we are, in the human condition, in our state as curious, sexual, inventive and loving beings, so that we "may have life and life to the full" (John 5).

Almighty God, our Father and our Mother in heaven,
thank you for the gift of our body and its sexuality.
Through the Resurrection of your son Jesus, help us to

heal our fear of and alienation from our body, help us to trust in the goodness of your creation. Help us to celebrate our sexual existence. Grant us the grace to integrate our sexuality into our drive for union with you for all eternity in heaven. Amen

THE GAY-FRIENDLY ATTITUDE OF JESUS AND THE EARLY CHRISTIAN COMMUNITY

All of us engaged in the spiritual dimension of gay, lesbian, bisexual and transgendered liberation constantly have had to deal with "Bible thumpers" who make the claim that the gay life-style is clearly condemned in the Bible as an "abomination" contrary to God's will. In his excellent book, *Gay Theology Without Apology*, Gary David Comstock makes the point that the Bible, written by men from within a patriarchal culture, is ridden with homophobia.

We can build a legitimate pro-gay sexual ethics based on our experience within the gay community and the direct, unmediated revelation that God's Spirit makes to us. I agree with Comstock that if it is true that Paul, for example, understands himself as unequivocally condemning homosexuality, then we must conclude that Paul was wrong in this judgment, just as we admit today that Paul was wrong in his acceptance of slavery. But it is my conviction that Paul understood all homosexual activity as acts undertaken by heterosexuals for the sake of lustful indulgence and had no idea of true gay love. The time has come for the Christian community to move beyond Paul's understanding of homosexuality.

I disagree, however, that we should just hand over the Bible to our enemies as many propose we should in the gay and lesbian liberation community. I will never forget my joy and sense of liberation when I first read John Boswell's critique of the traditional biblical passages used to condemn homosexuality (*Christianity, Social Tolerance, and Homosexuality* pp 91-117). I agree with Boswell that it can be established with good scholarship that nowhere in Scripture, the Old and the New Testament, is there a clear condemnation of a loving relationship between two adult gay men or two lesbians. I do not agree that to undertake such a scholarly task amounts to "apologizing" for those scriptural passages that on the surface appear to condemn homosexuality.

There are clear condemnations in Scripture of certain types of homosexual actions, such as rape, anal penetration of enemies as a sign of hatred, scorn, contempt and domination.

There is also a frequent condemnation of the use of sexuality in general and homosexuality in particular in religious fertility rites, for example, in such episodes as the Golden Calf (Exodus 32), the Flood (Genesis 6-9), and the destruction of Sodom (Gen. 19). It was a widespread belief among the pagans in biblical times that if one gave sexual pleasure to the pagan gods usually through the use of sacred prostitutes, both male and female, they would reward the worshippers with fertility for themselves, their animals and their fields. There is, as we have seen, an ongoing polemic in Genesis and Exodus against the use of sex in the worship of God, a polemic Paul continues in his attack on idol worshippers in Romans (1:18-22). The clear message in the Old Testament is that sex is in human hands to be used for human purposes.

But what Comstock seems to overlook is the possibility that despite the patriarchal and homophobic culture that Jesus was a part of, he and his followers did not share that prejudice. To be sure, this possibility is easy to overlook because centuries of homophobic redactors and translators have sought to eliminate all traces of this positive attitude.

A good example of this is the history of how the sin of Sodom, which even Jesus himself clearly understood as the sin of inhospitality to strangers (Luke 10-12) had been reinterpreted for political reasons as the sin of homosexuality. I have dealt with these negative biblical passages at length in my book *The Church and the Homosexual.*

We must, then, approach Scripture with what the feminists call "a hermeneutic of suspicion." Our suspicion is that, if there were a gay positive attitude on the part of Jesus and his followers, every effort would be made to bury the evidence. But, despite these efforts, certain gay positive elements remain in the New Testament. The first and remarkable element is the fact that nowhere in the four gospels did Jesus ever say one word of condemnation concerning homosexuality. This silence would be truly surprising if Jesus agreed in considering all homosexual relationships as seriously sinful. He makes very strong statements of condemnation for other human actions that he sees as necessarily contrary to the loving will of his Father in heaven.

THE BELOVED DISCIPLE

There are, I believe, at least three traces of a gay-positive attitude on Jesus' part in the New Testament. The first is the title that John the Evangelist gives himself "the Disciple whom Jesus loves." " Peter turned and saw the disciple whom Jesus loved following them—the one who had leant back close to his chest at the Last Supper and had said to him, 'Lord, who is it that will betray you'" (John 21:20-21). Notice what John writes. He does not call himself the disciple who loved Jesus; rather, he claims there was a distinct quality of the love that Jesus had for him that distinguished him from all the other disciples. And the other disciples did not dispute his claim.

John was the one who had the position of honor at Jesus' right at the Last Supper, and leaned his head on Jesus' chest. John was the one who stood at the foot of the cross with the women when all the other men fled in fear. And it was to John's care that Jesus committed his mother: "Seeing his mother and the disciple whom he loved standing near her, Jesus said to his mother, 'Woman, this is your son.' And then to the disciple he said, 'This is your mother!' And from that hour the disciple took her into his home" (John 19:26-27).

Again, it is John who is the first after the women to see the empty tomb and believe that Jesus had risen from the dead. Any one of you who have a gay sensibility will be keenly aware of the special nature of the relationship of love that reunites Jesus and John. In his old age, John is reported as telling the early Christian community, "Jesus had only one message! That you should love one another!"

THE GAY CENTURION AND HIS BELOVED BOY

No passages are clearer concerning the gay positive attitude of Jesus than the two accounts of Jesus' healing of the Roman centurion's servant as recounted in Matthew (8:5-13) and in Luke (7: 1-10).

> When he had come to the end of all he wanted the people to hear, he went in to Capernaum. A centurion was there who had a servant, a favorite of his, who was sick and near death. Having heard about Jesus, he sent some Jewish elders to him to ask him to come and heal his servant. When they came to Jesus they pleaded earnestly with him saying, "He deserves this of you, because he is well disposed toward our people; he built us our synagogue himself." So Jesus went with them, and was not very far from the house when the centurion sent word to him by some friends to say to him, "Sir, do not put yourself to any trouble because I am not worthy to have you enter under my roof; and this is why I did not presume to come to you myself; let my boy be cured by you giving your word. For I am under authority myself, and have soldiers under me; and I say to one man, 'Go' and he goes; to another, 'Come here' and he comes; to my servant, 'Do this' and he does it." When Jesus heard these words he was astonished at him and, turning round, said to the crowd following him, "I tell you, not even in Israel have I found faith as great as this!" And when the messengers got back to the house they found the servant in perfect health.

The words used in the Greek original of these texts for the centurion's servant are *entimos* and *pais*. These words could be translated as "my beloved boy" and would have clearly indicated to Jesus that he was dealing with two men in a loving homosexual relationship. Jesus expressed astonishment at he faith of the centurion and obviously moved by his love for his "beloved boy" heals the young man

A Roman Centurion was not allowed to marry during his period of service. Given the all-male nature of a Roman legion, the slave would have been the one to see to the physical comfort of the centurion himself. Slaves were not infrequently at the beck and call of the sexual pleasure of their master and it was not unusual for the relationship of a slave and master to grow into one of love.

Here we have the most direct encounter of Jesus with someday who would today be pronounced "gay" and Jesus' reaction was acceptance of the person without judgment and even eagerness to be of assistance to restore the "*pais*" to health, and by implication to fully restore the loving relationship of the two, making possible the renewal of any sexual activity which they would have enjoyed together prior to the illness.

It is important to note that Jesus does not exempt this gay relationship from the rest of what Jesus taught with regard to moral action, but rather, opens the possibility of bringing gay relationships within the compass of healthy and holy human love blessed by God.

In Matthew, when Jesus saw the Centurion, he saw someone who put the one he loved ahead of himself to the point of seeking the well-being of the *pais* at considerable cost to the Roman Centurion himself. After all, this proud representative of the military might of Rome had humbled himself out of love to beg a favor from an itinerant Jewish preacher. In Luke, Jesus heard of a Centurion who also put the *pais* ahead of himself, and, who practices justice and charity in his more general relationship with the Jewish community. These are both signs of all the attributes which Jesus had just presented in the Sermon on the Mount (Luke 6:20-38) and his definition of the "true Disciple" as one who hears his word and acts on it (Luke 6:47).

Any one who has been active in AIDS ministry is aware how often this totally unselfish gay love is played out in hospitals and clinics and homes all over the country when a gay lover is loyal to his dying companion to the end. According to the Roman law governing the possession of slaves, the Centurion was under no legal obligation to take care of a sick slave. His or her master could legally abandon a sick slave.

There is a final ironic note in the history of this passage. At every communion rite in the Roman Catholic Church, the last words that a communicant prays before receiving Holy Communion are: "Lord, I am not worthy to receive you, but only say the word and I shall be healed." I believe that God has a sense of humor and moved a Church prone to homophobia to use the faith confession of a gay man every time we receive the Lord in the Eucharist.

Jesus' Family of Choice

Some of the most tender human memories of Jesus described in the four gospels are those that depict him at home with his friends Martha, Mary and Lazarus in their home in Bethany. It is obvious that these people were Jesus' family of choice. "Jesus loved Martha and her sister and Lazarus" (John 11:5). The reason for that choice is also obvious. These people had an unconditional love for Jesus and had complete faith and respect for his mission. "Yes, Lord," Martha said, "I believe that you are the Christ, the Son of God, the one who was to come into this world" (John 11:27).

Jesus evidently did not receive such faith and respect from his biological family. In fact, we are told at one point that they thought he was crazy and intended to kidnap him and bring him home by force. "He went home again, and once more such a crowd collected that they could not even have a meal. When his relatives heard this, they set out to take charge of him, they said," He is out of his mind" (Mark 3: 20-21). All four gospels record Jesus as saying: "Who is my mother? Who are my brothers?" And stretching out his hands towards his disciples he said: "Here are my mother and my brothers. Anyone who does the will of my father in heaven is my brother and sister and mother" (Matt 12:46-50).We gather from the gospels that the house of Mary, Martha and Lazarus was Jesus' favorite resting place; he frequently went there to relax and be among friends. But who were the members of Jesus' family of choice? The first was Mary! Scholars no longer agree that this was the same Mary as Mary Magdalene who washed Jesus' feet with her tears at the supper at Simon's house. In Luke, (10: 38-42)

we are told the story of Martha inviting Jesus into her home
and becoming jealous of Mary "who sat at the Lord's feet
and listened to him speaking" while she was busy about
many things. The most striking passage portraying the deep
affection that existed between Jesus and Martha and Mary
occurs in the story of the resurrection of Lazarus, their
brother, from the dead. "Mary went to Jesus, and as soon
as she saw him, she threw herself at his feet saying, 'Lord,
if you had been here, my brother would not have died.' At
the sight of her tears, Jesus was greatly distressed, and with
a profound sigh he said, 'Where have you put him?'" (John
11: 32-34). There follows the astonishing story of Lazarus
who was Jesus' best friend being raised from the dead after
being buried for three days.

A second anointing just before Jesus' death is recounted
by John (12: 1-3). "Six days before the Passover, Jesus went
to Bethany, where Lazarus was, whom he had raised from the
dead. They gave a dinner for him there; Martha waited on
them and Lazarus was among those at table. Mary brought
in a pound of a very costly ointment, pure nard, and with
it anointed the feet of Jesus, wiping them with her hair; the
house was filled with the scent of the ointment."

We should note that Jesus' family of choice was very far
from the traditional Jewish family. First of all, they were a
family of three unmarried adults living together. This must
have been unusual since Jewish law required that all Jews
marry and procreate. Although Martha and Mary are referred
to as "sisters" and Lazarus is referred to as their "brother," we
should note that frequently in the Bible the words sister and

brother are used not to designate a biological relationship but to recognize a deep committed love relationship.

That leaves open the possibility that Jesus' family of choice was possibly a gay family; that Martha and Mary were lesbians and Lazarus was a gay man. In any case, Jesus' choice of family was not limited to the conventional and his value judgment had to do with the quality of the love that united the members, rather than their gender or sexual orientation. I am personally convinced that if Jesus were among us today, he might well choose to befriend a loving lesbian or gay couple and seek their company.

SCRIPTURAL CHARTER FOR THE INCLUSION OF LESBIANS AND GAYS

There is one passage in Scripture that I believe prophetically indicates that the Spirit of God is poured out in a special way on all those gay and lesbian Christians who are sincerely seeking to live their lives according to the teachings of Christ. This is the account of the baptism of the Ethiopian Eunuch in the Acts of the Apostles (8:26-39).

The Lucan author of this passage had as his purpose to depict the work of the Holy Spirit in the formation of the first Christian community and how that community differed from its predecessor, the Jewish community. He stresses that people who were considered outcasts by Israel for various reasons were to be included in the new community. One of these groups, symbolized by the Eunuch, includes those who for sexual reasons were excluded from the Old Testament community whose basis was a procreative covenant. "A man whose testicles have been crushed or whose adult male member has been cut off must not be admitted to the assembly of Yahweh" (Deut: 23:2).

However, in Isaiah (56: 3-4), there is an explicit prophecy that, with the coming of the Messiah and the establishment of the new covenant, the eunuch, who was formerly excluded from the community of God, will be given a special place in the Lord's house and an immortal name.

> No foreigner adhering to Yahweh should say, "Yahweh will utterly exclude me from his people."
>
> No eunuch should say, "Look, I am a dry tree."
>
> For Yahweh says this: To the eunuchs who observe my Sabbaths, and choose to do my good pleasure and cling to my covenant, I shall give them in my house and within my walls a monument and a name better than sons and daughters, I shall give then an everlasting name that will never be effaced.... These I shall lead to my holy mountain and make them joyful in my house of prayer. Their burnt offerings and sacrifices will be accepted on my altar, for my house will be called a house of prayer for all people. Lord Yahweh, who gathers the exiles of Israel declares: There are others I shall gather besides those already gathered.

This prophecy includes the homosexual because the term "eunuch" in the New Testament is used not only to mean those who have been physically castrated, but also in a symbolic sense, for all those who, for any reason, do not marry and bear children. For example, in Matthew 19:12,

Jesus, discussing marriage and divorce, says to his disciples: "There are eunuchs born so from their mother's womb; there are eunuchs made so by human agency; and there are eunuchs who have made themselves so for the sake of the kingdom of heaven."

The first category, that of eunuchs who have been so from birth is the closest description we have in the Bible of what we understand today as a person with a homosexual orientation. It should come as no surprise then that one of the first groups of outcasts of Israel which the Holy Spirit includes within the new covenant community is symbolized by the Ethiopian Eunuch, who is treasurer of the court of Queen Candice, the Queen of Ethiopia. The Eunuch, as was his practice, had made a pilgrimage to the temple in Jerusalem and spent his time there in prayer to Yahweh. As he was riding home along the road to Jericho, he was reading Isaiah, who predicts that after the Messiah comes there will be a special place in the house of the Lord for eunuchs who in place of progeny will be given an immortal life in heaven.

> He was now on his way home, and as he sat in his chariot he was reading the prophet Isaiah. The Spirit said to Philip, "Go up and join the chariot." When Philip ran up, he heard him reading Isaiah the prophet and asked, "Do you understand what you are reading?" He replied, "How could I unless I have someone to guide me?" So he urged Philip to get in and sit at his side, now the passage of Scripture that he was reading was this:
>
> *Like a lamb led to the slaughterhouse, like a sheep dumb in front of his shearers. He never opened his mouth. In his*

humiliation, fair judgment was denied him. Who will ever talk about his descendents, since his life on earth has been cut short?

The Eunuch addressed Philip and said, "Tell me, is the prophet referring to himself or someone else?" Starting, therefore, with this text of Scripture, Philip proceeded to explain the good news of Jesus to him.

Further along the road, they came to some water and the eunuch said, "Look there is some water here; is there anything to prevent my being baptized?" He ordered the chariot to stop, then Philip and the Eunuch both went down into the water and he baptized him. But after they had come up out of the water again Philip was taken away by the Spirit of the Lord and the Eunuch never saw him again but went on his way rejoicing (Acts: 6: 29-39).

The Eunuch rides into history "full of joy." I like to think of this eunuch as one of the first baptized gay Christians. It is obvious that what we are dealing with here is not just the story of an individual. The symbolism of the passage is quite obvious. The Holy Spirit takes the initiative in leading the new Christian community to include among its members those who were excluded for sexual reasons from the Old Testament community. Now that the Messiah has come there no longer is a need for every member of that community to procreate in the hope of fathering the Messiah.

Overcoming All Dualism

Paul speaks of the Holy Spirit eventually breaking down all the divisions that separate the human family one from another. Here the Holy Spirit prophetically takes the initiative to break down the division between straights and gays. We have the good fortune that we live in an age when that prophecy is being fulfilled by the gay liberation movement, which is a continuation of the initiative of the Holy Spirit. We can accept the Eunuch of the court of Queen Candice of Ethiopia as our first gay Christian brother in Christ and the apostle Philip as our special patron. And the judgment of the Spirit of God him/herself stands for all time. There is no reason why those who are sexually different cannot be received as fully qualified members into the Christian community.

We can conclude with certainty after recalling these four gay-positive episodes in the New Testament that homosexuality has not been condemned by the Church because Jesus condemned it, but because the Church inherited a condemnation of homosexuality from a secular world view expressed in many, if not all, cultures, which did not understand homosexuality and feared that which was different. The same question is before us today that was before the apostles: Are we ready to go forward in faith, with the Spirit's guidance overcoming the death-dealing attitude of the world which has exchanged "God's truth for a lie and has worshiped and served the creature instead of the Creator"? (Rom: 1:25) Will we let stand fear, hatred and ignorance of lesbian women and gay men who are our sisters and brothers in Christ? Will we deny them the place which Jesus evidently found for them in his proclamation of the good news? Or will we as faith communities seek to overcome our fears and prejudices, so long influenced by those of this world, to embrace the all-inclusive faith and freedom of the Gospels, which reaches forward to embrace all people without exception.

THE MASCULINE-FEMININE DIALECTIC AND ITS GAY SYNTHESIS

The crisis in the Roman Catholic Church and the Christian Church in general concerning sexual ethics, pedophilia and the role of authority, these and many other issues, are all surface manifestations of a deeper crisis the Church is undergoing. This deeper crisis has to do with the seismic shift going on in Western culture and in the world at large from the masculine to the feminine stage in the archetypal dialectic underlying our civilization. The Catholic Church with its all male celibate priesthood rapidly dying out, its insistence on hierarchical and authoritarian rule and denial of any democratic process or dialogue, its homophobia and suppression of woman, its insistence on absolute, objective truth and rejection of any subjective relative truth is the perfect example of the patriarchal society of old, a perfect manifestation of the now defunct exclusively masculine stage of the dialectic. With only dim awareness of this paradigm shift, the hierarchical Church is fighting tooth and nail to hold on to the old and prevent the coming of the new feminine phase of the dialectic.

My overview here of that dialectic owes a great debt to the book: *The Passion of the Western Mind: Understanding the Ideas that Have Shaped Our World View* by Richard Tarnas. I found this book by Tarnas, who is a philosopher and intellectual historian, to be one of the most insightful books in the field. Tarnas deals with the interplay of philosophy, religion and culture in the evolutionary development of Western civilization over the past three thousand years. Tarnas' insight is that this development has been an exclusive male phenomenon from start to finish.

The masculinity of the Western mind has been pervasive and fundamental in both men and women, affecting every aspect of Western thought, determining the most basic conception of the human being and the human role in the world. All the major languages within which the Western tradition has developed have tended to personify the human species with words that are masculine in gender. It was only within the last thirty years that our culture became consciously aware that the only words we have for all humankind were words that were masculine. In the past, the word "man" was felt to be uniquely capable of indicating a metaphorically singular and personal entity that is also intrinsically collective in character, a universal individual.

Within this cultural context, suppressing the feminine within them, men tended to feel superior to women. Most women, in turn, not being able to repress the feminine, internalized feelings of inferiority and inadequacy that they derived from the culture.

Tarnas makes the point that when gender-biased language is no longer the established norm, the entire cultural world view will have moved into a new era. The old kind of sentences and phrases, the character of the human self-image, the place of humanity in the cosmos and its nature, the very nature of the human drama, all will have been radically transformed. As the language goes, so goes the world view and vice versa.

An interesting example of this was the struggle between the American hierarchy and the Vatican in recent years to introduce a gender free version of the liturgy. The American bishops through dialogue with Catholic women became very sensitive to the pain exclusive male terms in the liturgy caused women and came up with a gender-free translation of the texts of the liturgy. When they sent these texts to Rome, the *feminaphobia* of the Vatican led them to suspect a feminist undermining of faith in the male God and they refused to allow the American Bishops to use a gender free liturgy.

THE MASCULINE AND THE FEMININE

The evolution of the Western mind is marked at every step by a complex interplay of masculine and feminine. There was a significant partial reunion with the feminine corresponding to every great creative watershed of Western culture, for example, the great openness to the feminine in the personality of Jesus. Many of the great saints and founders of religious movements were extraordinarily open to the feminine.

A striking example is described in William Meissner's book, *Ignatius of Loyola: The Psychology of a Saint*. Meissner identifies the transformation of Ignatius from a

soldier and *bon vivant* to a mystic, a saint and the founder
of a religious order with his experience of the feminine
dimension of himself.

> To a large extent, the feminine aspect of [Ignatius']
> character played the dominant role in his mysticism,
> reflected in his yearning for love, his intense affectivity, his
> passivity and submissive yielding to the divine embrace,
> and the overwhelming experience of copious tears to the
> point of physical disability. I have suggested that at some
> level his spiritual absorption may have its psychic roots in
> the yearning of the abandoned child for its lost mother.

THE INTERNAL MASCULINE DIALECTIC

Tarnas notes, also, that there is an archetypal polarity
within the masculine itself. On the one hand, the masculine
principle (again in both men and women) involves what
might be called the Promethean impulse: restless, heroic,
rebellious and revolutionary, individualistic and innovative,
eternally seeking freedom, autonomy, change and the new.
On the other hand, there is the Saturnian impulse which is
both complement and opposite to the Promethean impulse:
conservative, stabilizing, controlling, dominating, that
which seeks to sustain order, contain and repress. This is the
juridical-structural-hierarchical side of the masculine that
has expressed itself in patriarchy.

> The two sides of the masculine—Prometheus and
> Saturn, son and father—are implications of each other.

Each requires, calls forth, and grows into its opposite. On a broad scale the dynamic tension between these two principles can be seen as constituting the dialectic that propels "history" (political, intellectual, spiritual). It is this dialectic that drives the internal drama through out The Passion of the Western Mind, the unceasing dynamic interplay between order and change, authority and rebellion, control and freedom, tradition and innovation, structure and revelation. I am suggesting, however, that this powerful dialectic ultimately propels and is propelled by—as it were, in the service of—yet another overarching dialectic involving the feminine or "life."

WHY THE MASCULINE STAGE HAD TO COME FIRST

This development of the masculine archetype with the repression of the feminine did not occur because women are less intelligent than men; nor is it due solely to social constrictions placed on women. The "man" of the Western intellectual tradition can be seen as a socially constructed "false universal," as some feminists claim, the use of which both reflected and helped shape a male-dominated society. With this understanding of male domination, some feminists have as their agenda to deconstruct this "socially constructed false male universal" and assert a socially constructed feminine "she" model in its place, replacing men with women, a father God with a Goddess, the male quest for autonomy and freedom with a feminine quest for symbiosis and merging into the feminine divine matrix.

Rather, we are dealing here with something much more profound and necessary than a mere substitution. It is my belief that we are dealing here with what Jung named the *anima/animus mundi*, the Spirit of God, who is working out an evolutionary dialectic. Its past thesis was the development of the masculine archetype, which for mysterious reasons had to be accomplished first; its present and future antithesis will be the working out of a feminine archetype, which will not contradict or repress the masculine, but eventually result in the synthesis of an androgynous fulfillment of all humans, male and female.

I suspect that the historical priority given to the working out of the masculine archetype has something to do with the greater power and closeness to life and nature of the feminine. If the feminine archetype had been worked out first, the masculine development, which is much more fragile, could never have occurred or taken place only with extreme difficulty. Now we can no more simply return to the divine maternal matrix, than an adult can find fulfillment by returning to the mother's womb.

The "man" of the Western tradition has been a questing hero, a Promethean biological and metaphysical rebel, who has constantly sought freedom and progress for himself and who has thus constantly striven to differentiate himself from and to control the matrix out of which he has emerged. The Promethean hero has been present in both men and women. The evolution of the Western mind has been driven by a heroic impulse to forge an autonomous, conscious, rational self by separating it from the primordial unity with nature. The result of that process has been the transcendent self, the independent individual ego, and the self-determining human being in its existential uniqueness, separateness and freedom.

All my previous writings, especially the book *Freedom Glorious Freedom: The Spiritual Journey to the Fullness of Life for Gays, Lesbians and Everybody Else,* have been solidly within that evolutionary process of liberation. The final stage of the masculine liberation into "Freedom, Glorious Freedom" for both men and women has to do with spiritual liberation into an independent stance vis-à-vis the divine and a separation off from the collective identity with the institutional church.

Freedom of conscience expresses the direct, unmediated access of the Promethean individual to the divine in a free, direct and personal relationship of love. The gay liberation process of "coming out of the closet" is another Promethean journey into autonomy and authenticity. As Maurice Blondel said: "Our God dwells within us, and the only way to become one with that God is to become one with our authentic self."

The balancing feminine moment has to do with building a loving spiritual community and achieving a deep passionate relationship of personal love with each other and with the divine, a relationship built not on any submersion of our ego and identity into any collective matrix, but built instead on a relationship and a community freely entered into by free, autonomous, independent and self-determining individuals.

The question must be asked: Why has the pervasive masculinity of the Western and spiritual tradition suddenly become so apparent to us over the past few years, while it remained invisible and unconscious to almost every previous generation? It is only through the feminist movement in the last thirty years that we have become conscious of how exclusively masculine, for example, our common prayers and liturgies were. Hegel once made the observation: "The owl of Minerva spreads her wings only at the falling of dusk!" Every civilization is unconscious of itself until it reaches its death; and it is only in the dying stages that it becomes fully conscious of what it is all about. True wisdom can be achieved only at the end point. The three thousand year masculine tradition of Western civilization is reaching its apogee; it has been pressed to its utmost one-sided extreme in the consciousness of the late modern mind.

The crisis of modern humanity is an essentially masculine crisis. As we have seen, the evolution of the Western mind has been founded on the repression of the feminine, "on the repression of undifferentiated unitary consciousness, of the participation mystique with nature, a progressive denial of the *anima mundi,* of the soul of the world, of the community of being, of mystery and ambiguity, of imagination, emotion, instinct, body, nature and women.

Today men and women face the existential crisis of being solitary and mortal conscious egos thrown into an ultimately meaningless and unknowable universe, an environment that is increasingly artificial, mechanistic, fragmented, soulless and self-destructive. The evolution of the masculine archetype has reached an impasse. If we continue on this one-sided dialectic, the human race faces the real possibility of self-destruction through nuclear warfare or widespread environmental collapse. Humans are feeling progressively isolated, alienated from their communities, from nature and from each other. Robert Bellah has explored this alienation in his book *Habits of the Heart*. This separation from the feminine necessarily calls forth a longing for a reunion with that which has been lost. There is an enormous felt need to rediscover and honor the feminine in all its dimensions.

Tarnas believes that the resolution of this crisis is already occurring in the tremendous resurgence of the feminine archetype in our culture. He sees this phenomenon as visible in the rise of the feminine, the growing empowerment of women and the widespread opening up to feminine values by both men and women. He sees further evidence of its emergence in the rapid burgeoning of women's scholarship and gender-sensitive perspectives in virtually every intellectual discipline, especially in the fields of theology and spirituality. Most of the best theology being written today is coming from the hands of women like, to name but a few, Carter Hayward, Elizabeth Johnson, Rosemary Reuther. It is seen in an increasing sense of unity with the planet and all forms of nature on it, in the increasing awareness of the ecological and the growing reaction against political and corporate policies supporting the domination and exploitation of the environment, in the growing embrace of the human community and the collapse of long-standing political and ideological barriers separating the world's people, in the deepening recognition of the value and necessity of partnership, pluralism, and the interplay of many perspectives. As Tarnas says:

> The deepest passion of the Western Mind has been to
> reunite with the ground of its being. The driving impulse

of the West's consciousness has been its dialectical quest not only to realize itself, to forge its new autonomy, but also, to recover its connection with the whole; to come to terms with the great feminine principle in life, to differentiate itself from but then rediscover and reunite with the feminine, with the mystery of life, of nature, of soul. And that reunion can now occur on a new and profoundly different level from that of the primordial unconscious unity, for the long evolution of human consciousness has prepared it to be capable at last of embracing the ground and matrix of its own being, freely and consciously. The *telos*, the inner direction and goal, of the western mind has been to reconnect with the cosmic in a mature participation mystic, to surrender itself freely and consciously to the embrace of a larger union that preserves human autonomy while also transcending human alienation.

THE ROLE OF MARY, THE MOTHER OF JESUS

One interesting manifestation of the feminine archetype that Tarnas cites was the papal declaration in 1950 of the *Assumptio Mariae*, that the body and soul of Mary, the mother of Jesus, had been taken up into heaven at the moment of her death, an anticipation of the ultimate resurrection of all the faithful. The healthy role of Mary in Catholicism has always been to reveal the repressed feminine face of God, the dimension of mercy, love, compassion, tenderness and concern. This became very necessary when the patriarchal image of God the father was one that evoked fear, guilt,

and shame, and when Church authority had subordinated
compassion to the law. The image of Mary as revealing the
maternal dimension of God was expressed beautifully in the
popular prayer the *Memorare*:

> Remember O most gracious Virgin Mary
>
> That never was it known
>
> That anyone who fled to thy protection,
>
> Implored thy help, or sought thy intercession
>
> Was left unaided.
>
> Inspired by this confidence,
>
> I fly unto thee, O Virgin of Virgins, my mother,
>
> To thee I come,
>
> Before thee I stand sinful and sorrowful.
>
> O Mother of the Word incarnate
>
> Despise not my petition,
>
> But in your mercy hear and answer me. Amen.

The symbolism of the Assumption places male and
female persons as equal in the domain of heaven.

THE PROVIDENTIAL ROLE OF GAY MARRIAGE

THE BREAKDOWN OF THE STEREOTYPE OF HETEROSEXUAL MARRIAGE

Many healthier women today, who are more in touch with both their masculine and feminine dimension and see themselves as whole persons, are increasingly unwilling to play the role of being the mediators of feminine emotional and compassionate needs of men. They want a man who is a total human person in himself! They are demanding, and rightly so, that we men get deeply in touch with our own feminine dimension. Much of the more positive side of the men's movement has been seeking to open the male psyche to the feminine values of emotion, intuition, and compassion. Many men, in turn, who are becoming in touch with both the masculine and feminine dimensions of themselves are refusing to continue to play the role of being the mediators of the masculine needs of women for assertiveness and autonomy. It is this shift in consciousness that has caused the enormous amount of breakdown and divorce when heterosexuals try, with the Church's encouragement, to follow the traditional patterns of male dominance and female submission—and refuse to recognize the equality of the sexes. Both genders are being called on to develop the fullness of their own humanity, so that they can approach each other as complete, independent persons and not remain essentially dependent on the other gender for their completion.

THIS IS NOT THE APOCALYPSE

Fundamentalist and other Christians, sensing that we are at the end of an era and that a radical change is taking place, are tempted to think that we have arrived at the age of the apocalypse and the Second Coming. Most apocalyptic writings are tinged with a pathological religious fear. They have more to do with the worship of Baal than the God revealed by Jesus. The truth the fundamentalists sense is the world, as they know and understand it, is coming to an end. I, too, believe that we have come to an end of an era, but this is not a time to run off to a mountain. It is a time to stay in the marketplace and reach out to your neighbor with compassion and genuine love. Then, if the Rapture comes, you will be ready for it. But chances are that human history in God's providence has a long future still ahead.

Tarnas concludes his book with the statement that the restless inner development and incessantly innovative masculine ordering of reality characteristic of the Western mind has been gradually leading, in an immensely long dialectical movement, toward reconciliation with the lost feminine unity, toward a profound and many-leveled marriage of the masculine and feminine, a triumphant and healing reunion. "Our time is struggling to bring forth something new in human history. We seem to be witnessing, suffering, the birth labor of a new reality, a new form of human existence, a 'child' that would be the fruit of this great archetypal marriage, and that would bear within itself all its antecedents in a new form."

> This stupendous Western project should be seen as a necessary and noble part of a great dialectic, and not simply rejected as an imperialistic-chauvinist plot. Not only has this tradition achieved that fundamental differentiation and autonomy of the human, which alone could allow the possibility of such a larger synthesis; it also painstakingly prepared the way for its own self-transcendence. Moreover, this tradition possesses resources, left behind and cut off by its own Promethean advance, that we have scarcely begun to integrate and that, paradoxically, only the opening to the feminine will enable us to integrate. Each perspective, masculine and feminine, is here both affirmed and transcended, recognized as part of a larger whole, for each polarity requires the other for its fulfillment. And their synthesis leads to something beyond itself; it brings an unexpected

opening to a larger reality that cannot be grasped before it arrives, because this new reality is itself a creative act.

Judy Grahn, in her brilliant book, *Blood, Bread, and Roses*, holds a theory identical to that of Tarnas:

> The male tradition has the "way" to sally forth in a straight line, and women (led to a great extent by feminists) have successfully followed men out of the strangling subjective matrix of the past. But men's undeviating path has also led us away from the old truths and over a cliff, without "the way back." It is the women's tradition that holds the memory of the way back.
>
> We need all the tools of humankind, arrow and loom, hierarchy and consensus, competition and cooperation, tenderness and ferocity, leisure and discipline. Men and women are not in deadly opposition. They are dancing the steps that give us human culture… I believe the emergence of the Gay community in the twentieth century also signal a crossing, especially with the connection of lesbians to female centrality and "flow."

THE LESBIAN AND GAY ROLE IN THE GREAT DIALECTIC

Thirty-five years ago, in 1968, the gay Christian movement began as a visible, organized presence in the human community, with the creation of Metropolitan Community Church, followed two years later by Dignity for gay Catholics, and many other Christian gay groups.

In his preface to the French translation of my book on gay spirituality, *Taking a Chance on God,* Father Jacque Perroti, a leader in the gay Christian movement in France, speaks of this new era as a *declic,* a special moment in history, "a revelation of the slow emergence of a positive homosexual identity from the heart of the world. After so many ages of rejection, destruction and intimidation, a wind of freedom began to blow!" I am convinced that gay liberation is a central part of the great dialectic of human liberation that God is working out through Her/His Holy Spirit. I will deal here with the special role that lesbians and gays have to play in that dialectic. Scripture tells us: "Without a vision the people will perish!" Gay people have a special need for a vision of their role in bringing about the reign of God in history to sustain them in the difficult battles that lie ahead.

To my surprise, Tarnas makes no mention of the emergence some thirty-five years ago of a positive gay identity on all levels—social, political, cultural, and spiritual—all over the world. This emergence, I believe, has a teleological purpose in the development of the *anima/animus mundi.* This presence of a visible lesbian and gay community, for the first time in my knowledge in the past three thousand years, is an integral part of this dialectic and another aspect of the rediscovery of the feminine or, what I prefer to call, the balancing of the masculine and feminine in a new synthesis in the human personality.

Clearly, the dominant dialectic of the masculine archetype, with its repression of the feminine, has also included the repression of the homosexual. G. Rattrey Taylor in his book *Sex in History* has pointed out that patriarchal culture combines a subordinationist view of women with a strong repression of homosexual practices; cultures based on a matriarchal principle, on the other hand, tend to combine an enhancement of the status of women with a relative tolerance of male homosexual practices.

The rise of the feminine dialectic in recent years gives us reason to hope that gays and lesbians will be fully accepted in the future human community. At the heart of all male homophobia is a *feminaphobia* and repression of the feminine. Gay men are seen as a threat to patriarchy because they frequently are in touch with and act in accord with the feminine dimension of themselves. So the evolution of the feminine archetype potentially brings with it gay male liberation. And if it is true, as feminists tell us, that lesbians are persecuted because they are women who refuse to play a subordinate role to men and not because they are lesbian, then they too will experience liberation with the rise of the feminine archetype.

However, even if it were possible to achieve, merely adopting the new feminine archetype and repressing the masculine would not represent any improvement in the human condition. In such a world, gay men would continue to be oppressed, not because of their openness to the feminine, but because of their maleness, just as in this patriarchal culture lesbians are persecuted not primarily because of their lesbianism but because they are women. And there is the possibility that lesbians would continue to be oppressed because of their openness to the masculine.

THE SEED OF SYNTHESIS

A better alternative is the emergence of a visible group that can live out fully both its masculine and feminine dimensions without the need to repress either. We need a group that will model the ideal goal of humanity's present evolution: people who can keep their masculine and feminine dimensions in good equilibrium and can bring forth a balanced synthesis of the two. This, I believe, is the providential role of the gay and lesbian political and spiritual groups that through divine providence have come into being over the past thirty-five years; and this is an important aspect of the masculine and feminine dialectic that Tarnas missed. Every dialectical movement toward a higher synthesis, if it is to succeed, must carry the seed of its resolution within itself.

We who are lesbian or gay must have a vision and be clear about what special gifts we bring to this moment in history. Feminists, who insist that lesbians should devote all their energy to women's liberation and not to gay liberation, are shortsighted because they fail to understand, or consciously reject, the concept of the dialectic. Instead of a "both/and" understanding of the relation of the masculine archetype to the feminine, they adopt an "either/or" understanding, substituting the development of the feminine archetype and the repression of the masculine.

For example, some feminist theologians believe that it is necessary to drop a belief in Christ and Christianity because Christ is biologically male. Christianity is seen as hopelessly wedded to patriarchy, male privilege and the repression of the feminine. And, of course, every troglodyte pronouncement of the Vatican against the feminist movement (for example, the denial of the right of women to be ordained to the priesthood) seems to prove their point. Consequently, they advise lesbians to drop out of gay spiritual organizations such as Dignity, Integrity and MCC and devote themselves exclusively to the women's liberation movement.

I am convinced that the institution of patriarchy has contaminated Jesus Christ's message of equality and love —by male privilege and by the repression of the feminine and by homophobia. The time has come to cleanse ourselves and throw off these aberrations. Gay spiritual groups, I believe, are leading the way for the whole Church to bring about this transformation.

Clearly, after three thousand years of oppression, the feminist movement, still in its adolescence, must of necessity contain a rejection of the masculine archetype in order to purify and grasp the feminine in all its richness. We are at the moment when the feminine archetype's antithetical moment in the dialectic is in ascendance. This is the time for the feminine to assert its equality and dignity and to achieve its separation from, and independence of, the masculine.

However, I believe that within the gay community both of us, gay men and lesbians together, have a role to play in human history, a role that could be seriously jeopardized if we should begin to conform to an either/or understanding of masculine and feminine archetypes.

THE NEED OF IMMORTALITY

A few years ago, my friend and colleague Mary Hunt, a lesbian theologian, spoke about the traditional Christian belief in resurrection of the body and immortality. She agreed with Rosemary Ruether that in feminine consciousness there is no need for individual immortality. Women can be satisfied with the idea that at death they will become symbiotic with the great feminine matrix in the hope that, although their ego-identity is lost, new life will rise from that matrix.

I believe there is a partial truth in this position. Because of their physical participation in birth, many women stay closer to nature and seem more at ease with the natural process of birth, maturing and death. If they have children, they can be more inclined to find their immortality in their offspring, rather than in their own achievements. Many of us who are male do have something to learn about accepting life's processes with peace and equanimity from our sisters. But many of us, especially those without children or the possibility of children, are especially open to this message in Scripture:

> No eunuch should say, Look, I am a dried-up tree.
>
> For Yahweh says this: "To the eunuchs who observe my Sabbaths
>
> And choose to do my good pleasure and cling to my covenant,
>
> I shall give them in my house and within my walls
>
> A monument and a name better than sons and daughters;
>
> I shall give them an everlasting name that will never be effaced." (Isaiah 56:3-5)

I disagree with Mary Hunt's belief that this masculine desire for personal immortality is pathological. On the contrary, I believe that men's and women's desire to escape the limits of death and aspire to personal immortality is healthy. This desire falls into the category that the philosopher Maurice Blondel explored of human needs that are necessary for human fulfillment and impossible by human means alone. Consequently, the desire for immortality opens us up to our need for the power and the grace of the divine.

Winning for us this divine gift of personal immortality was the Promethean task undertaken by Jesus. Perhaps this task does represent a desire present in a more pronounced way in the masculine archetype and perhaps it can be opposed to the feminine archetypal drive to seek merger into the undifferentiated. This difference could be one reason why the masculine dialectic had to come first. We had to achieve the ultimate levels of freedom and autonomy of the masculine archetype in order to be able to relate to God, not through symbiosis in the divine matrix, but in a free relationship of love. In the words of Pierre Teilhard de Chardin, "Must I again repeat the truth, of universal application, that, if it be properly ordered, union does not confound but differentiates."

The desire for personal immortality is certainly not exclusively confined to men. Every human being who has had the experience of deep personal love can find that desire in his or her own heart. Every love song ever written speaks about being "eternally" yours. Stoic philosophers urged their followers never to fall in love, because lovers always desire immortality for themselves and their lover and such a desire in irrational. We are all called into a personal relationship of love with the divine and death cannot destroy that personal relationship. On the contrary, our individual personal identity will continue beyond death for all eternity. This triumph over death is a special gift from God, which lies totally beyond our human power. At the same time, this gift responds to a profoundly felt need in the human heart.

A MOMENT OF REGRESSION

Let me illustrate what the role of the gay community is in this dialectic with a recent instance of a momentary failure of this dialectic and a reversion to the exclusively masculine archetype. During the intense debate over lifting the ban on gays in the military in 1993, I was struck by the many similarities between this debate and the debate that went on in Germany in the late twenties concerning the sodomy laws. As I described in my book *The Church and the Homosexual,* Hitler's Nazi party was well aware of the association between non-violence and male homosexuality. In the late 1920s, there was a strong gay rights movement in Germany. The movement succeeded in 1928 in persuading the German government to send a letter to all Germany's political parties asking for their position on the reform of paragraph 175 of the German criminal code, a sodomy statue. The Nazi reply was as follows:

Munich, 14 May, 1928

Community before Individual

It is not necessary that you and I live, but it is necessary that the German people live. And they can only live if they

can fight, for life means fighting, and they can only fight if
they maintain their masculinity. They can only maintain
their masculinity if they exercise discipline, especially in
matters of love.... Anyone who even thinks of homosexual
love is our enemy. We reject anything that emasculates
our people and makes them a plaything of our enemies,
for we know that life is a fight, and it is madness to think
that men will embrace fraternally. Natural history teaches
us the opposite. Might makes right. And the stronger will
always win over the weak. Let us see that we once again
become the stronger.

The Nazi party's reply began with an either/or
proposition, either the individual or the collective. Their
fascist choice of the collective over the individual, surprisingly
enough, represents a rejection of the Promethean male
archetype in favor of the feminine. The political philosophy
that lay behind that judgment was a despair of building a
democratic community based on the loving commitment of
individual citizens. Again we are dealing here with a half-
truth: the individual's rights must always be in balance in
relation to the common good. As one wit put it: "The rights
of my fist end at the tip of your nose!"

What the Nazi party wanted to gain was a total collapse
of all individual rights into the collective need of the people,
as they interpreted that need. The essential Christian message
concerning the value of the individual is that each one of us
has a unique, unmediated relation to the divine: "In truth I
tell you, in so far as you neglected to do this to one of the least
of these, you neglected to do it to me!" (Matt: 5:45) Every

one of us, then, has a value that is greater than that of the species or "the people." "It is better," the Sanhedrin judged, "for one man to die for the people" (John: 18:14). There is a deep lesson here, that we can never legitimately subordinate the intrinsic value of the individual to the collective.

While listening to the debate over gays in the military, I heard over and over again the same message coming from the military as sent by the Nazis. The super macho aggressive male self has to be maintained for the sake of the state. In fact, the Nazi debate was more honest; the issue was not sexual; the issue was love. A deep human love between members of the same sex, this was the Nazi's enemy. "It is madness to think that men will ever embrace fraternally."

In 1936, Heinrich Himmler issued a decree which said: "Just as we today have gone back to the ancient German view in the question of marriages mixing different races, so too in our judgment of homosexuality—a symptom of degeneracy that could destroy our race—we must return to the guiding Nordic principle, extermination of degenerates." Orders were given that homosexuals were to wear pink triangles. In 1937, the SS newspaper Das Swartze Korps estimated that there were two million homosexuals in Germany and called for their extermination. Himmler gave orders that all known homosexuals were to be sent to level three concentration camps—that is, death camps. As far as we know some two hundred thousand gays were worked to death in these camps.

The fight over the armed forces policies has deep political and social manifestations. I do not want to feed gay paranoia by making us feel that we are as vulnerable today as we were at the time of the Nazis in 1928. The feminist liberation movement has begun the process of the dialectic; and gays are in a new, much more advanced place now. In fact, our enemies are much more frightened than we and have gathered all their forces to try to deny the right of marriage to gay people. The enormous anti-gay campaign going on today, fomented by the religious right with the full cooperation of the Vatican, is clear evidence that they are fearful that they are losing the battle. And with good reason; a whole world is disappearing and it necessarily has to disappear. We must be ready, however, for another moment of backlash. We must have a vision of where our movement of gay liberation is going and of what we can do both for ourselves and the rest of humanity, our brothers and sisters, for we are involved in a process of liberating all human beings to the fullness of life. This is the work of the Holy Spirit who is fundamentally at work in gay liberation and in the development of our gay spirituality, which is based first of all on equal love, the love of equals for each other, so that brothers can embrace fraternally and sisters embrace in a sisterly way.

THE SPECIAL GIFTS THAT GAYS BRING TO THE DIALECTIC

What are these special gifts, then, that the lesbian and gay spiritual community will bring to the evolutionary process, the great dialectic between the masculine and the feminine? Tarnas makes a very strong point that the process, if it is to succeed, must retain all the gains of the past three thousand years of the development of the masculine thesis, especially the free and autonomous individual self.

In his book, *The Archetype and the Collective Unconscious,* Jung discusses some positive aspects of male homosexuality that he had become aware of in the course of his clinical work: "This (homosexuality) gives them a great capacity for friendship, which often creates ties of astonishing tenderness between men, and may even rescue friendship between the sexes from its present limbo of the impossible." Our first task, then, is to witness to deep bonds of love that exist between gay men and lesbians and to develop deep bonds of loving friendship between gay men and their lesbian sisters. We must model a kind of love based on equality and respect for each other as equal subjects and no longer based on domination and submission.

Since I do not speak from within a lesbian perspective, I must leave the corresponding observation to my lesbian sister, Mary Hunt. In her book *Fierce Tenderness,* she makes the point that women, once they overcome any feelings of inferiority or inadequacy as women, can make an extraordinary contribution toward building human communities based on ties of friendship rooted in equality. Just imagine the strength with which new communities built on such bonds of friendship and equality would have to remedy so many of the desperate problems we face today. Problems spawned by poverty, unemployment, racism, alcohol and drug abuse, depression, the break up of families and crime would not go untended in such communities.

As I reported in *The Church and the Homosexual,* Pierre-Claude Nappey many years ago posed what I believe is the essential question for understanding homosexuality. The fruitful question is not from whence homosexuals come, but where are they going—or, better, for what purpose do they exist? "The question is not is homosexuality excusable owing to the particular circumstances of the individual concerned, but whether it is an integral part of the much vaster behavior pattern of the collectivity and whether it contributes in some way to its proper functioning."

The particular importance of that question lies in the fact that human sexual activity participates in the radical freedom of the person. Whatever participates in human freedom can only be understood adequately in terms of a teleological goal or purpose, a movement toward some ideal goal. Consequently, it is only by posing the question why, for what purpose, that we can hope to arrive at an adequate understanding of the human phenomenon of gay and lesbian orientation. For only by finding the answer to the teleological question can we detect in what sense homosexuality can be part of the great dialectic between the masculine and the feminine archetypes being worked out in history under the guidance of the Holy Spirit. As Nappey observed: "Homosexuality must be seen... as corresponding to a definite finality. My own feeling is that not only is it possible for homosexuality to be of equal value with heterosexuality in individual cases, but that it has over-all significance and a special role to play in the general economy of human relations, a role that is probably irreplaceable."

I believe that no more urgent task faces gay liberationists than determining that finality. For on its discovery depends both the ability of homosexuals and lesbians to fully accept themselves with true self-love and understanding and the ability of heterosexual society to accept a homosexual minority, not just as objects of pity and tolerance at best, but as their equals, capable of collaborating in the mutual task of building a more humane society.

The Collective Role Of The Homosexual Minority

What, then, is the collective role of the homosexual minority in human society? And under what circumstances can that potential contribution become a reality? We have a clue to that role if we consider the frequently dehumanizing and depersonalizing role that prevailing gender-identity images play in our culture. We can summarize the objectionable stereotypes as follows: Men in our culture are supposed to be strong, tough, assertive, objective, courageous, logical, constructive, independent, unsentimental, unemotional, aggressive, competitive, diligent, disciplined, levelheaded, controlled, practical, promiscuous and persuasive. Women, in turn, are expected to be weak, passive, irrational, emotional, empty-headed, unassertive, subjective, illogical, dependent, fitful, devoted, self-effacing, impractical, artistic and receptive. Commenting on these stereotypes Dr. Elinor Yaknes observes that gender-identity is "the result of programming. Aside from the different physiology and anatomy.... I cannot think of any property that is uniquely the property of either sex."

If we assume that these heterosexual gender identity images constitute the total mature content of the human personality, serious consequences follow. They result in a tendency to see the human individual, whether male or female, as essentially partial and incomplete. No human person is seen as complete in him- or her-self, but as essentially dependent on the opposite sex for her or his completion. The insights that have come from the women's liberation movement have made us aware of the depersonalized and unequal status of women in our culture. And since heterosexual men receive their identity usually from their relationship with women, they in turn also suffer a depersonalized and partialized self-image.

One of the consequences of identifying with the heterosexual identity images proffered by our culture is that the only type of relationship that remains possible is a type of master-slave relationship, wherein the male seeks to dominate the female and the female seeks to be dominated. This kind of relationship leads to enormous amounts of repressed anger. And since anger is the primary anti-aphrodisiac, most heterosexual marriages in American culture cease being sexually fulfilling after a short period.

It is precisely this understanding of direct personal relationships based on inequality of the sexes that led the young Hegel to despair of solving the problem of human unity on the personal level of interpersonal love. He was led to seek the political solution for true community in the unifying collective concept of "citizen." He felt that it was only by taking your identity from the state and identifying with the depersonalized concept of citizen that humans feel equal to each other. This formed the basis of the Nazi idea of subordinating the individual to the state. Marx, for similar reasons, turned to class identity, "Member of the Proletariat," to escape the same dilemma.

Richard Mohr in his book *Gay Ideas*, suggests: "Male homoerotic relations, if institutionalized in social ritual, provide the most distinctive symbol for democratic values. Democracy, Mohr argues, will be grounded only when male homosexuality is not just tolerated, as something begrudgingly given rights, and not just accepted, as something viewed as an indifferently different life-style, and not just prized, as one admirable thing among many. Democracy will be firmly grounded only when male homosexuality is seen and treated in social ritual as a fundamental social model. Here again we are dealing with a fundamental contribution of homosexuals to the political future of humanity.

SAME SEX MARRIAGE

As I write these pages, the media are celebrating or decrying the Massachusetts Supreme Court ruling that gay couples have the right to marry. Once again we must ask why gay marriage, which was unthinkable just a few years ago, should suddenly be at the center of media attention. Once again, I believe that this is providential. Gays have an important gift to make to the human community in modeling out a new and different style of interpersonal relations based on equality and there is a desperate need for this understanding of marriage on the part of all—gay and straight alike.

On the theological level, true Christian love, even married love, can exist only between persons who see themselves as somehow total and equal to each other. Christian love must be love out of fullness and not out of need. It is not only the complementariness of the other sex that attracts but also the fact that, while I sense that complementarity, I can at the same time sense that here is a being who is whole and entire in himself (or herself) and… worthy of standing beside me and entering my life as an equal. The gender stereotypes mentioned above negate any possibility of such a personal relationship for any heterosexual who takes them seriously.

John Boswell, a church historian, for his book *Same-Sex Unions in Pre-Modern Europe*, discovered that the Church did not celebrate marriage as a sacrament until 1215. Until then the Church viewed marriage as a civil contract. One bought a wife and the wife was the buyer's property. There cannot be a sacrament unless a relation of love is involved. It was not until the twelve hundreds and the Romantic Movement that marriage began to be seen as based on a love relation.

However, gay union rituals were universally found in Church documents as early as the fourth century. Boswell argues that these rituals were true marriage ceremonies. Such ritual celebrations of marriage were possible because gay couples saw each other as equal and based their relation on interpersonal love. In other words, nine centuries before heterosexual marriages were declared a sacrament, the church liturgically celebrated same-sex covenants.

Usually in these rituals, the story of the two gay martyrs, Bacchus and Serge, was told. These two men were third century gay lovers and soldiers in the Emperor's guard. They converted to Christianity. The Emperor ordered them to offer him worship as a god, but they refused saying that they had no God but Jesus. The Emperor, in order to disgrace them, stripped them of their military garb, dressed them as women and marched them through the streets of Rome. They were delighted and sang love songs to each other. The Emperor then ordered them to be imprisoned and had Bacchus tortured to death in front of his lover Serge. Serge was told that he would go to the same death if he did not repent and offer worship to the Emperor. That night in his cell he began to waver, but Bacchus in glory appeared to him in a dream and told him: "Do not hesitate to go to your death, and I will be your reward in heaven!" In other words, not only did the early Christian Church see same-sex love as holy and worthy of sacramental celebration, they also saw that love as a love that would continue on for all eternity in heaven.

Priest-psychologist Eugene Kennedy points to the same creative role of the homosexual in relation to the heterosexual community. He writes of the beneficial consequences of a greater acceptance of homosexuality in society, so that the process leading to our gender identity and sexual orientation will be based less in fear of nonconformity and more in a challenge to be true to the authentic self.

When humans can face with less fear the complex of feelings and impulses that are part of each person's sexuality, they will be able to accept and integrate their experience into a less prejudiced and more creative self-identity. That is to say, when persons can be more friendly toward what really goes on inside them, they will feel less pressure to deny or distort their experience of themselves;

the achievement of their masculine or feminine identity will be less the acceptance of a rigidly imposed social stereotype and more the attainment of a multi-dimensional truth about themselves. Greater openness to self can only increase our chance of more successful gender identity.

Traditionally, the married relationship between males and females found its support and stability in social roles, custom and laws which made relatively secondary the type of direct personal relationships between the parties involved. But all these social supports are rapidly fading away. Clearly, genuine personal love between husband and wife as equals will be necessary to sustain the heterosexual family.

If the homosexual community were allowed to play its role with full acceptance, homosexuals would cease to play their past negative role of undermining marriage relationships into which they have been forced by their desire to escape detection. Nearly half of all divorces approved by Church courts are based in the homosexuality of one or the other partner. Instead, they could be a help in leading society to a new and better understanding of interpersonal love between equals—rather than the role playing of tradition—as the foundation for the marriage relationship.

Over a hundred years ago in a particularly prophetic passage, poet/mystic Rainer Maria Rilke had this to say about the changing role of women:

> We are only just now beginning to look upon the relationship of an individual person to a second individual objectively and without prejudice, and our attempts to live

such associations have no model before them.... The girl and the woman, in their new, their own unfolding, will but in passing be imitators of masculine ways, good and bad, and repeaters of masculine professions. After the uncertainty of such transitions it will become apparent that women were only going through the confusion and the vicissitudes of these disguises in order to cleanse their own characteristic nature of the distorting influence of the other sex.... The humanity of women, born in full time in suffering and humiliation, will come to light when she will have stripped off the conventions of mere femininity in the mutation of her outward status.... Some day there will be girls and women whose name will no longer signify an opposite to the masculine, but something in itself, something that makes one think, not of any complement or limit, but only of life and existence: the feminine human being. This advance will change the love experience, which is now full of error, will alter it from the ground up, reshape it into a relation that is meant to be of one human being to another, no longer of man to woman. And this more human love (that will fulfill itself, infinitely considerate and gentle, and kind, and clear in binding and releasing) will resemble that for which we are preparing with struggle and toil, the love that consists in this, that two solitudes protect, border and salute each other.

THE SPECIAL GIFT OF CREATORS
OF THE BEAUTIFUL

The second attribute that Jung assigns to gay men is an aesthetic sensitivity to beauty. "He (the homosexual) may have good taste and an aesthetic sense which are fostered by the presence of a feminine streak." One of the greatest revelations that God is making of herself to the world is through beauty. In the words of Augustine: "Late have I loved you, O Beauty, ever ancient, ever new. Late have I loved you!" I particularly like this name, "Beauty," for God because it is genderless. Gay people are indeed extraordinarily open to beauty. There is no doubt that homosexual men are often freer to develop aesthetic values than heterosexual men. These men, living out the heterosexual stereotype, cannot be open to beauty and are fearful and ashamed if they show any sensitive response to beauty. Yet one of the most powerful revelations that God makes of herself is through beauty.

Gay men, then, have important roles to play in guiding humanity to a deeper appreciation of aesthetic values. (This was the theme of the television program *Queer Eye for the Straight Guy*.) There is an extraordinary amount of glory given to God by the creation of beauty that comes from the gay community. One of the great tragedies of the AIDS epidemic is that so many of our talented gay brothers have been dying before they completed their life's work.

THE GIFT OF COMPASSIONATE SERVICE

The third attribute that Jung assigns to gay men is: "He may be supremely gifted as a teacher because of his almost feminine insight and tact!" The attraction of many if not most gay men to service roles, where they have been particularly successful, has gone relatively unnoticed by our culture, since in the past men in these roles were obliged to remain hidden in the closet. The gift of compassion is one of the gifts gay men receive almost simultaneously with their gayness. This is a gift that gay men should be especially grateful for. Everywhere I go, if I find a tactful, insightful, sensitive man engaged in compassionate human service, working as teacher, as minister, with the sick, the retarded, the blind, the disabled or children, more often than not, he is gay.

PRESERVERS OF TRADITION

Another positive effect that homosexuality can have on men, according to Jung, is their "feeling for history" and their relative tendency "to be conservative in the best sense and cherish the values of the past." Since the majority of traditional values have their basis in the heterosexual family structure, Jung's observation seems rather paradoxical. In fact, to the radical right the homosexual appears as a threat to the family structure and, as a consequence, a threat to all those values traditionally associated with it. However, most of those traditional values represent customs, mores and taboos imposed from without to which the majority gives uncritical conformity. Forced by their sexual orientation to live for the most part outside those structures, self-accepting gay people are thrown back on themselves and their own experience in order to reestablish those values which merit their acceptance. Almost in direct proportion as they are cut off from traditional patterns, they must seek out and recreate the real values which these patterns were meant to convey and must preserve them by their personal commitment.

THE GIFT OF SPIRITUAL LEADERSHIP

Jung's final, surprising observation concerning the positive aspects of homosexuality has to do with the religious and spiritual development of humanity. "He (the gay person) is endowed with a wealth of religious feelings which help him bring the *ecclesia spiritualis* into reality, and a spiritual receptivity which makes him responsive to revelation." If we take this observation of Jung's seriously, then there is no serious question about the worthiness of gay men to be ordained ministers.

The spiritual process gay men go through of accepting their exile status in this world and giving up the myth that we can find our ultimate meaning exclusively in this world can result in great spiritual freedom. This freedom can help gay men to live fearlessly and authentically in this world. By deepening their spiritual life, they can turn what many see as the curse of gayness or the curse of being a social outcast into spiritual gold.

Matthew Kelty, a Trappist monk and spiritual advisor to Thomas Merton, speaks of this aspect of gayness in his book *Flute Song Solo: Reflections of a Trappist Hermit*:

> Sometimes I wish I were more like others. I am aware
> of a difference; some insight into things; some capacity for
> the poetic and the spiritual, which, if not exceptional—and
> it is not—is still strong enough to set me off from others.

Nor do I hesitate to say that this has some relationship with homosexuality. For though I have never practiced it, I am aware of an orientation that is as much in that direction as the other; further, that given the knowledge, the opportunity, the circumstances, I could easily as not, have gone in that direction. But people of my kind are often so placed, the reason, as I have worked it out, that they are more closely related to the "anima" than is usual.... What such people yearn for is solace in their solitude and an understanding of their fate, their destiny.... The man with a strong anima will always experience some inadequacy until he comes to terms with his inner spirit and establishes communion, no small achievement. Until then he cannot act truly as a complete person, since he is not one. He will then be unable to relate in depth to others. The unhappy experience of many is that they are unable to relate to others, not aware that their problem is a lack of communication with themselves. The blind comfort the blind, but they cannot open each other's eyes.... Perhaps a healthy culture would enable them so gifted by God or nature (i.e. homosexuals) to realize their call and respond to it in a fruitful way.

What then must gay people do to transform their curse into a blessing? If we find time each day to spend in God's presence in prayer, we will develop a living affectionate, personal relationship with God. We will then be able to recognize all the broken events in our lives—the losses, the pain and the grief—as connected and given meaning by the great events of God's redemptive work in Jesus. If we pray daily then God will give us the grace to be fully prepared for death. But if we enter freely into the presence of God every day, how easy it should be, for those of us who have already mourned and let go of the myth of finding our meaning by belonging to this world, to enter once and for all into the presence of divine love at the moment of death. *Maranatha*! Come, Lord Jesus, Come!

CONCLUSION

The Holy Spirit is working deeply in the history of the world to bring about the reign of God. This reign includes the establishment of justice and peace in history itself in this world. To participate in this dialectical process, we are at a critical moment when both men and women must incorporate and open themselves up to the feminine archetype in a very real synthesis with the positive accomplishments reaped from the three thousand year history of the development of the masculine archetype.

In his letters, Paul speaks of the Holy Spirit working in the world to help us overcome all divisions that separate us from each other, and, therefore, cut us off from the fullness of ourselves (Gal: 3:28). The only way I can become fully one with myself is to be one with all humanity without exception, no racial exceptions, no gender exceptions, no exception because of sexual orientation. Don't forget that Jesus' name for himself was "son of man" or, as we would say today, "son of humanity."

Paul names three great divisions that remain to be overcome through the reconciling work of the Holy Spirit. The first is the overcoming of the master/slave division, including the overcoming of slavery of all kinds, the fullness of political freedom for all humans. This task is still going on.

The second division Paul mentions is the division between Jew and Greek; by that he symbolizes all divisions based on race, nationality, ethnicity, and religion. The Holy Spirit will work in the world to undo all these divisions so that we will all understand each other as brothers and sisters of every human being that exists and not feel any separation because of racial, religious or ethnic difference.

The final division that must be overcome is the difference between male and female. We must become equals and become one with our brothers and sisters outside ourselves. And in so doing, we can become one with the feminine and the masculine in ourselves.

Overcoming those divisions is a very slow historical process that has been going on over centuries. But today, I believe, the gay liberation movement has emerged out of the heart of the world to play a decisive role in overcoming this final division. Again, let us remember that Scripture says that the stone that was rejected will become the cornerstone. Gay spiritual communities are being called by God to play that "cornerstone" role. The only way, however, that we can play that role is to overcome our fears and have the courage to come out of the closet. Gays must model in a very public way their ability to balance the masculine and feminine dimension within themselves, their ability to put together genuine human love for each other with a deep spiritual life and their deep awareness of the presence of the Holy Spirit in their life. They must become, therefore, "candles on the hilltop" for everyone to see.

This cornerstone role is a real challenge. But you can be certain that, if you are lesbian or gay, the Holy Spirit is calling you to take some steps in that direction, to be more open about your gayness and to be more open about the depths of your spiritual life. We must seek God's help because a cornerstone, after all, is a small but essential part of a building, the entirety of which is the work of the Holy Spirit. The Spirit waits on our freedom to invite her in to make use of our gifts and talents in bringing about the reign of God, a reign of justice and peace, a reign where God's glory is achieved through the fullness of life that all humans share, gay and straight alike. "The glory of God are humans fully alive."

EPILOGUE:
OBJECTIVE DISORDER

Since his election as Pope Benedict XVI, the former Cardinal Ratzinger, has carried the persecution of gays and lesbians to almost a hysterical level. Just out of the gate as Pope, one of his first actions was to fire the famous Jesuit editor of America, Thomas Reese, for having the temerity, among other things, to publish an article which suggested that the Church should reconsider its attitude on homosexuality. Benedict has ordered Catholic adoption agencies in the United States to close their doors rather than cooperate with State-mandated laws to help gay couples adopt children. He has challenged all laws approving gay marriage and ordered the American bishops to support the constitutional amendment to ban gay marriage. One image an editor of a Catholic publication suggested to me is that of the Pope shouting at the water as the tide comes in. I would like to reflect here on one action in particular: the implications of the Instruction forbidding the ordination of self-accepting gay men to the priesthood.

In that Instruction the Vatican has given a vicious collective slap in the face not only to gay priests and seminarians, but to every gay, lesbian, bisexual, transsexual and transgendered person on the earth. The Instruction, issued by Pope Benedict XVI, calls homosexual orientation an "objective disorder" and any sexual action that flows from that orientation is contrary to the divine will and profoundly sinful. Note that this judgment applies not only to seminarians and clergy struggling to live in accordance with their imposed vow of chastity, but to all lesbian women and gay men. Any effort by a gay person to reach out for human sexual love, no matter what the circumstances, is judged as evil. Scripture says that if anyone loves, they know God because God is love. The Vatican says that if gay people enter into a human sexual love relation, they know evil and will separate themselves from the love of God.

I foresee two probable consequences to this Instruction; the first will be a sharp decline in the candidates for the priesthood. That decline has already reached a critical point in Europe and the United States. In fact, the Instruction may well deal a death blow to a cultic priesthood of exclusively chaste male (heterosexual or repressed homosexual) men and force the hierarchy to open the priesthood to other candidates such as married men and, eventually, to women. If this happens, it represents what I call the "shrewdness" of the Holy Spirit.

It is common knowledge that the primary yet unstated reason for the publication of this Instruction is the priest/

child abuse scandal that has seriously and probably permanently damaged the Catholic Church's moral authority. This document has little to do with God or even morality. This is a political document issued in self-defense by the human and sinful hierarchy of the institutional church. The hierarchy, rather than accept their responsibility for this crisis, decided to scapegoat gay priests and seminarians. Starting with the fact the vast majority of the victims were young boys, some officials in Rome and many in the United States declared that the majority of the perpetrators were homosexual priests. They assumed without evidence that every same sex act implies homosexual orientation. In fact, most empirical research evidence points to the opposite conclusion. The majority of men involved in child abuse are heterosexual. The motivation of most child abusers is not sex but power.

A more probable explanation for the abuse, according to the vast majority of psychologists is the high number of priests who were immature, insecure about their tendencies and full of doubt and guilt. Any homosexual who achieves a healthy self acceptance and has a positive attitude towards his sexual orientation is precisely the one this Instruction excludes from the seminary and ordination, whereas those gay men who are struggling with immaturity and self-rejection because of their homosexuality, who are full of doubt and guilt—they are acceptable candidates for seminary. The healthy are unacceptable; only the pathological may apply. Rather than setting up a cure of the child abuse crisis, this Instruction guarantees that the crisis will continue. What is bad psychology has to be bad theology.

The second consequence of this Instruction will be a further decline of the moral authority of the hierarchy. The Instruction is so out of touch with reality that it is obvious that the authors consulted only so-called experts who agreed with its dogmatic premises that homosexual orientation is an orientation to evil. On November 30, 2005, the Vatican newspaper published a commentary on the Instruction written by Fr. Tony Anatrella, a French priest and psychoanalyst, and a consultant to the Pontifical Council for the Family. Father Anatrella's essay is such a homophobic caricature of gay priests as to be laughable. Yet Vatican spokesmen say Anatrella's essay does represent an official explication of what the Instruction's authors had in mind. By limiting themselves to such prejudiced consultants the Vatican cut itself off from the reality of gay life. Every major psychological association has concluded from empirical evidence that homosexuality as such does not imply psychological disorder and homosexuals can be as mature and responsible as heterosexuals. The Vatican has an important role in the human search for truth, but it certainly does not have the right to *invent* the truth concerning homosexuality.

The Vatican is right, I believe, in claiming that we are dealing with an "objective disorder." But that objective disorder has nothing to do with homosexuality but with the Vatican itself. One clue to what that disorder is can be found in the use of the word "objective." Traditionally, the Vatican viewed all homosexual behavior as a choice motivated by lust by otherwise heterosexual men and, therefore, "subjectively disordered." But when modern psychologists accumulated undeniable evidence that there is such a thing as homosexual orientation that is not chosen and is unchangeable, the Vatican was forced to concede that homosexual orientation, since it is not a matter of choice, cannot be qualified as subjectively morally evil. One possible conclusion then was that homosexual orientation was part of God's creative plan and since " *agere sequitur esse*," the acts that would flow from such an orientation, if they are in the context of interpersonal love, would be morally acceptable. To say that God created humans with an orientation to evil is blasphemy. In defense of its tradition the Vatican chooses to go the other way. God intended all humans to be heterosexual. Homosexual orientation must represent, then, some mysterious disruption of God's plan possibly due to original sin. The orientation itself is an orientation to evil and any action flowing from that orientation would be sinful.

There is a deeper reason why the Vatican seems so out of touch whenever it deals with sexual ethics. Paradoxically, the Vatican, which teaches the Christian position that God is love, has no adequate philosophical foundation for dealing with love, divine or human, or with the unique individual person and that person's subjective consciousness. The Vatican remains exclusively committed to objective Thomistic realism and has systematically rejected any effort to introduce the human subject into its moral reasoning. In his encyclical *Veritatis Splendor*, published in 1993, Pope John Paul II defended this choice because objective realism makes possible the formulation of absolute, universal laws essential to the power and absolute authority of the Church, whereas to introduce the human subject is to allow a kind of relativism, which would undermine the absolute authority of the Church. On several occasions Pope Benedict has identified this "relativism" as the worst intellectual enemy of Church authority. For over a hundred years, progressive Catholic theologians have urged the Church to develop its philosophical foundation to allow for the unique human subject, the person, and that person's contribution to theological thinking. Instead of basing its sexual morality on biology, gender differences and procreation, this would allow the Church to deal with the specific human purposes of sex such as interpersonal love and companionship, but the Church has adamantly refused to do so.

As far back as 1893, Maurice Blondel, in his book *L'Action,* argued that objective realism, since it could only deal with conceptual reality, was necessarily depersonalized and depersonalizing because the unique individual person can never be objectified in a concept. He also maintained that love is a human experience that can only be known from within in the action of loving. He believed that a philosophy that included the unique human person would be much more compatible with Christian belief. For Blondel, "will-willing" represents the total potential in the human will; "will-willed" is whatever portion of that potential we have actualized through our choices and actions to date, i.e., what we *could* will versus what we *have* willed. The ultimate level of truth was not the conformity of human concepts with objective reality but the conformity of will-willing with will-willed.

That truth can only be arrived at through human action and commitment and is a truth that is only available subjectively in individual consciousness.

Jesus at the Last Supper told his followers, "It is necessary that I go away. If I do not go away the Spirit can not come to you. But if I go away I will send you the Spirit. The Spirit will dwell in your hearts and lead you into all truths." Jesus was recommending a spiritual maturing process by which his followers' contact with God would no longer be Jesus outside themselves but the divine life living within them.

"Because I have said these things to you, sorrow has filled your hearts. Nevertheless, I tell you the truth, it is to your advantage that I go away. For if I do not go away, the Holy Spirit will not come to you, but if I go, I will send him to you. When the Spirit of truth comes, he will guide you into all the truth" (John: 16:6-3).

Jesus is expressing the need in some way to prove to be a fallible leader in order for his followers to mature and move on to the next stage in their spiritual life, where their authority is no longer just Jesus outside themselves but the Spirit dwelling in their hearts.

As Blondel put it, what Jesus was promising was not a *"visio beatificans,"* a purely intellectual viewing of the divine essence, but a *"vita beatificans,"* a sharing on the subjective level of divine life, a sharing that can rise up into our consciousness when we place an action of love. "For God is love and if anyone loves they know God." "The only way we can know God is in some way to be God, to share in divine life." When we place an action that is in conformity with that divine spirit dwelling within us then we experience total certainty and intense joy and fulfillment.

A central Christian teaching based on the indwelling of the Spirit, one that is without doubt of utmost importance especially to those who are gay or lesbian, is the teaching of freedom of conscience. This teaching was expressed anew in a powerful way in the documents of Vatican II:

> *Every human has in his or her heart a law written by God. To obey that law is the dignity of the human. According to that law we will be judged. There we are alone with God whose voice echoes in our depths.*
>
> (The Pastoral Constitution of the
> Church in the Modern World)

According to this teaching, where do you seek to find out what God wants of you? You turn inward in prayer and you listen carefully to discern what your heart is saying to you. You ask God, if you are about to make a choice, if what you are about to do is in harmony with God's spirit dwelling in your heart, to fill your heart with confidence, peace and joy. "Lord, grant me the grace to know your will for me and the courage to be able to do it." Note that God speaks to us primarily though our hearts, that is to say, through our emotions and only secondarily through our reason. This indwelling of the Holy Spirit was the grounds on which Ignatius Loyola based his Spiritual Exercises, especially his Rules for the Discernment of Spirits. (This is the reason why the Vatican never trusted the Jesuits and preferred Opus Dei's rigid authoritarianism instead.)

Paul saw the gift of the Holy Spirit on Pentecost Sunday as fulfillments of this prophesy of Jeremiah:

> *"This is the new covenant I will make with my people in those days. I will put my law within them, and I will write it on their hearts and I will be their God and they shall be my people. No longer will they teach one another, or say to each other: Know the Lord. For they shall all know me from the least to the greatest," says the Lord! (Jeremiah 31:31-34)*

Again Paul quotes these words from the prophet Joel:

> *"In the last days, it will be," God declares, "that I will pour out my Spirit on all flesh, and your sons and daughters will prophesy and your young men will see visions. And your old men will dream dreams. Even upon slaves, both men and women, I will pour out my Spirit and they shall prophecy."*
> *(Acts 2: 16-17)*

(There is no comment on these passages in John Paul II's encyclical, *Splendor Veritatis*, which gives a brilliant defense of the role of reason in moral life.) The hierarchy has no exclusive claim to discerning what the will of God is. This power belongs to every baptized Christian who has received the Holy Spirit.

The Church is in need of a special transformation to become a Church of the Holy Spirit. With the coming of the Spirit, we, like the Apostles, must give up the security of a provident leader. We have a special need with God's grace to become mature, self-motivated, autonomous people, no longer dependent on outside forces for a sense of our identity and well-being. We must not let our enemies outside ourselves define us; we must let the Spirit of love that dwells in our hearts define us. If we approach external Church authorities, it should not be to seek an approval they cannot, and frequently will not, give us. Rather, it should be to witness to what the Holy Spirit is saying through our experience.

The loss of the moral authority of the Catholic Church is truly tragic. There is a desperate need for that authority in such issues as poverty, war and peace, the economy, healing the environment and many other areas. True authority in the Church of the Holy Spirit will only be exercised by leaders who are tuned in and listening to what the Holy Spirit is saying in and through the experiences of the people of God. Here is where God is making an ongoing revelation of God's truth. In the Book of Revelations, the Holy Spirit makes the statement: "Behold! I am doing something new." Paul in Romans 4:17 writes "The Spirit is calling into being what does not now exist." Scripture and reason are not the only sources to reveal to us the will of God. We also have the living and creative voice of God's Spirit speaking to us directly in our hearts and through our experiences. And Jesus promised us that if we prayerfully listen to that voice the Spirit "will lead us into all truth."

For twenty-five years, I conducted ecumenical retreats twice a year at Kirkridge Retreat Center located in the Poconos, for gay and lesbian Christians using the theme

"Seeking Intimacy with God." Every Saturday night during the weekend retreat we held a session called the "fishbowl" during which ten selected retreatants shared their spiritual journey as gay men or lesbians. After hearing five hundred such biographical accounts, a clear pattern of how the Holy Spirit acts in gay people emerged. Initially, there was a period of acceptance of homophobic Church teaching which led to self-loathing, emotional breakdown, alcohol and/or drug abuse and relating to God purely out of fear. More often than not there were heartbreaking experiences of being thrown out and disowned by their family and Church community, being abused and beaten by fellow students in school, attempted suicide and coming close to despair. The amount of human suffering in the gay community was overwhelming. In the midst of all that suffering and despair the Spirit came to them and touched their hearts. They became aware that God loved them as gay men or lesbians. This experience of God's love healed their spirit and psyche. Having accepted themselves as loved by God, they were then able to reach out for companionship. "It is not good that a human remain alone. Every human needs a companion of his or her own kind" (Gen 2:5). The final stage in that journey was a call to ministry, the Spirit urging them to share their experience of God's love and all the good things that God has done for them with their brothers and sisters. Gay seminarians should keep in mind that Jesus was not a priest in his Church. His authority to minister came directly from the Spirit of God dwelling in his heart.

Wherever humans are being liberated to a greater fullness of justice and life, there is God's Holy Spirit "doing something new" in establishing the kingdom of God on earth. The two great liberation movements of our day, women's liberation and gay and lesbian liberation, are both the work of the Holy Spirit. And they are not unconnected. The root cause of all homophobia is what I name *feminaphobia*, the hatred of all things feminine. This is the most central "objective disorder" in the Vatican.

The Holy Spirit cannot be contained. "The wind of the Spirit blows where it will!" I do not think it was pure coincidence that the movie *Brokeback Mountain* was released simultaneously with the Vatican Instruction. That movie is a revelation of the human goodness and beauty of gay love that speaks directly to the human heart. Another event that happened in that same time period was the release of *Saint of 9/11*, a documentary on the life of the gay Franciscan priest, Mychal Judge, the chaplain of the New York fire department who was killed on that fateful date. Father Judge, a gay man, was the perfect model of a saintly priest. Again I think it was no coincidence that at the very moment Father Judge was dying while anointing a fallen fire fighter at the foot of the World Trade Towers, hierarchs were drafting the Instruction in Rome banning gays from the priesthood.

Father Jacques Perotti, a leader of *David and Jonathan,* the Christian gay movement in French speaking countries, speaks of a *declic*, a special moment in history, "a revelation of a positive homosexual identity from the heart of the world. After so many ages of rejection, destruction and intimidation, a wind of freedom has begun to blow!" Since this is the work of God, no human force can stop it.

APPENDIX

An Open Letter to the U.S. Conference
of Catholic Bishops on the Issue of
Homosexuality, November, 2000

*The following is the letter Mel White
attached to his Festschrift essay.*

In 1974, the delegates of Dignity's first national convention requested in a letter, that a dialogue be opened between the American bishops and the members of the Catholic gay and lesbian community. With very few exceptions that letter was ignored.

Now, nearly thirty years later, once again I call upon the American bishops to open that dialogue.

For over thirty years, I have ministered as priest and psychotherapist to lesbians and gays. I helped found Dignity, New York to provide a safe and loving community within the Catholic Church for gay people. This June will mark the twenty-fifth year I have given retreats for lesbians and gays, at Kirkridge, an ecumenical retreat center.

I have written three books on gay spirituality: *The Church and the Homosexual, Taking a Chance on God,* and *Freedom, Glorious Freedom.* I also published an autobiography on

my own spiritual journey as a gay priest. As a result of
my experience, I have come to the conclusion that what is
at stake at this point in time is not only the spiritual and
psychological health of many gay and lesbian Catholics and
other lesbian and gay Christians. What is at stake is your
moral authority to teach on this issue.

In the past, when you undertook a listening process to
hear what the Holy Spirit was saying through the People
of God, you won our respect. We respected you when you
made your statements on the economy, on nuclear warfare
and, especially, your aborted effort to draw up a letter on
the role of women in the Church. You listened carefully to
what women had to say and, and drew up your statements
responding to what you heard from women. These actions
gave us gay and lesbians reason to hope that the Holy Spirit
would lead you into a spirit of willingness to listen to us gay
and lesbian Catholics.

What is at stake now is your own moral authority!
Unless we gay and lesbian Catholics receive the message that
you take us seriously and are willing to listen carefully to
what the Holy Spirit is saying to you through our lives and
our experience, your judgments on homosexuality will be,
for the most part, ignored and you will lose what authority
you have left to deserve to be listened to with respect on this
issue.

I have never heard the same level of courage from the
American Bishops in dealing with the Vatican as that shown
by the Major Superiors of Religious Men in response to
the egregious document issued by The Congregation for

the Defense of the Faith entitled, "Some Considerations Concerning Homosexual Persons" as follows:

"We view (this document) as a hindrance to the Church leaders of the United States in this most difficult and sensitive area of human living… We are shocked that the statement calls for discrimination against gay men and lesbian women. We find the reasoning for supporting such discrimination to be strained, unconvincing and counterproductive to our statements and actions to support the pastoral needs and personal dignity of such persons. Far from a help to the Bishops and other religious leaders in the United States Catholic Church, the statement complicates our already complex ministry to all people.

"Moreover we find the arguments used to justify discrimination based on stereotypes and falsehoods that are out of touch with modern psychological and sociological understandings of human sexuality. We regrets such actions by the CDF and we reaffirm our support for the human rights of all our brothers and sisters."

As a gay Catholic theologian and psychotherapist, I am fully aware of the enormous destruction recent Vatican documents have caused in the psychic life of young Catholic gays, and of the violence they will provoke against all gay people. I find myself in a dilemma what kind of faith and trust can I place in a teaching authority that I see clearly acts in an unloving, hateful and destructive way toward my gay family and is more interested in defending its institutional interest than it is in truth and justice?

In the name of the thousands of gay and lesbian Catholics and other Christians to whom it has been my God-given privilege to minister, I make this statement:

At this point, the ignorance and distortion of homosexuality, the use of stereotypes and falsehoods in official Church documents, forces us who are gay Catholics to issue the institutional Church a serious warning. Your ignorance of homosexuality can no longer be excused as inculpable; it has become of necessity a deliberate and malicious ignorance. In the name of Catholic gays and lesbians everywhere, we cry out "Enough!"

Enough!

Enough of your distortions of Scripture. You continue to claim that a loving homosexual act in a committed relationship is condemned in Scripture, when competent scholars are nearly unanimous in acknowledging that nowhere in Scripture is the problem of sexual acts between two gay men or lesbian women who love each other, ever dealt with, never mind condemned. You must listen to biblical scholars to find out what Scripture truly has to say about homosexual relationships.

Enough!

Enough of your efforts to reduce all homosexual acts to expressions of lust, and your refusal to see them as possible expressions of a deep and genuine human love. The second group you must listen to are competent professional psychiatrists and psychotherapists from whom you can learn about the healthy and positive nature of mature gay and lesbian relationships. They will assure you that homosexual orientation is both unchosen and unchangeable and that any ministry promising to change that orientation is a fraud.

Enough!

Enough of your efforts through groups like Courage and other exgay ministries to lead young gays to internalize self-hatred with the result that they are able to relate to God only as a God of fear, shame and guilt and lose all hope in a God of mercy and love. What is bad psychology has to be bad theology!

Enough!

Enough again, of your efforts to foster hatred, violence, discrimination and rejection of us in the human community. We gay and lesbian Catholics pray daily that the Holy Spirit will lead you into a spirit of repentance. You must publicly accept your share of the blame for gay murders and bashing and so many suicides of young gays and ask forgiveness from God and from the gay community.

Enough, also, of driving us from the home of our mother, the Church, and attempting to deny us the fullness of human intimacy and sexual love. You frequently base that denial by an appeal to the dead letter of the "natural law." Another group to whom you must listen are the moral theologians who, as a majority, argue that natural law is no longer an adequate basis for dealing with sexual questions. They must be dealt with within the context of interpersonal human relationships.

Above all else, you must enter into dialogue with the gay and lesbian members of the Catholic community. We are the ones living out the human experience of a gay orientation, so we alone can discern directly in our experience what God's spirit is saying to us.

And for the first time in history you have gay and lesbian Catholic communities of worship and prayer who are seeking individually and collectively to hear what the Spirit is saying to them in their gay experience: what experiences lead to the peace and joy of oneness with the Spirit of God and what experiences lead away from that peace and joy!

God gave you the commission of discerning the truth. But there is no mandate from Jesus Christ to "create" the truth. We pray daily that the Holy Spirit will lead you to search humbly for the truth concerning homosexuality through dialogue with your lesbian sisters and gay brothers.

The only consolation I can offer gay and lesbian Catholics in the meantime is the profound hope that the very absurdity and hateful spirit of recent Vatican documents will lead gay Catholics to refuse them and recognize the contradiction of their message and that of Jesus who never once spoke a negative word concerning homosexuals.

I work, hope and pray that lesbian and gay Catholics and other gay Christians will exercise their legitimate freedom of conscience, discerning what God is saying to them directly through their gay experience. I hope, too, that they will be able to de-fang the poisons of pathologically homophobic religion, accepting the good news that God loves them and accepts them as gays and lesbians and refusing to be caught in the vortex of self-hatred vis-à-vis a God of fear.

I believe that we are at the moment of a special *"kairos"* in this matter. The Holy Spirit is "doing something new." I was recently the guest at a gay ecumenical community that established homes for adult retarded people in the city of Basel in Switzerland. The extraordinary spirit of love and compassion that permeated that community was a foretaste of what lies in the future. I believe there is a vast reservoir of human and divine love that has remained until now untapped because of prejudice and homophobia. The Spirit is calling on you to help release that vast potential of human and divine love through your action sat this national conference.

Please be assured that the actions of Soulforce and Dignity at your national conference are based in profound respect and love. We pray and hope that the same Holy Spirit who has graciously liberated us who are gay to self-respect and self-love will liberate in you, our Catholic leaders, a profound love for your gay brothers and lesbian sisters and melt away all prejudice and judgmentalism in your hearts. May you make us welcome as full members in your family in Christ.

May God bless your efforts!

Sincerely in Christ,
John J. McNeill
10/19/2000

HOW SHOULD LESBIAN AND GAY CATHOLICS RESPOND TO THE HIERARCHY'S DECISION TO BAR GAYS FROM THE SEMINARIES AND THE PRIESTHOOD?

The following is a talk John McNeill gave to Dignity/
Chicago on the occasion of receiving the Tom Dooley Gay
Alumni Award from Notre Dame University in October 2005.

On September 21st, I read in the New York Times that the Vatican, under Pope Benedict, the former Joseph Ratzinger of the Congregation for the Doctrine of the Faith, is considering the decision to bar all gays, even celibates, from the priesthood. My immediate reaction was great sadness for the Church I love, then rage at the injustice of it all and then painful awareness of all those good and holy gay men in the priesthood who will feel betrayed and abandoned by their Church. I then entered into prayer and asked the Holy Spirit to help me discern what this is all about.

First, the Spirit assured me that this decision has nothing to do with God or the teaching of Jesus Christ. Notice the total absence of any sense of love and compassion for all the suffering this will cause gay Catholics generally and gay priests especially. The hierarchy is aware that the child abuse crisis has seriously undermined their authority and power. This purge is a political move by the sinful human church to try to repair the damage done to their power and prestige by scapegoating the gay members of the clergy. They ignored all the expert advice from psychologists that gayness was not the cause of the child abuse crisis. By this move they are trying to avoid their responsibility for the crisis and any need on their part to reform the Church.

The Holy Spirit is still ultimately in charge of the Church and will call the shots on how the Church will evolve and be transformed and our task as gay Catholics is to prayerfully discern what the Holy Spirit is about in this moment of crisis and support that transformation.

I shall never forget the excitement we felt at the first meeting of New York Dignity some 35 years ago. We had put a small notice in the Village Voice. We had hoped for a few people. But over a hundred people crowded into the room we reserved at Good Shepherd Church in Gramercy Park. Obviously, we were meeting a strongly felt need in the Catholic lesbian and gay community. I remember saying at that first meeting: "Dignity is not something that we can give ourselves, but with God's grace, it is something that we can give each other!"

We had a simple plan: To bring the message of God's love to gay, lesbian, bisexual, transgendered and transsexual people. Secondly, by giving witness to the presence of the Holy Spirit in our lives, we hoped to enter into dialogue with the institutional Church to bring about a change in its teaching on homosexuality; a change fully justified by our new understanding of scripture, tradition and of human psychosexual development. Our cry here was that "what is bad psychology has to be bad theology and vice versa." The evidence is in that those who try to live out Church teaching on homosexuality frequently destroy their mental health and submit themselves to worshipping a God of fear. In Paul's words: "You were not called to a spirit of slavery to let fear back into your lives again, you are called to a spirit of adoption. You have the right to call your God, *Abba* (Daddy)."

We were full of the hope and enthusiasm of Vatican II, which had redefined the Church as "The People of God." Our naïve hope that the Church would change seemed confirmed a few years later in 1976, when my book *The Church and the Homosexual*, which seriously challenged Church teaching, was given an *imprimi potest* by the General of the Jesuits, Pedro Arrupe (an action for which he paid heavily later by being deposed as General by the Pope) and I was granted permission to publish.

Now almost thirty years later, although the Holy Spirit has abundantly blessed our ministry to bring the message of God's love to our sisters and brothers, I am sorry to have to report that in terms of dialogue with the hierarchy, it has been mostly downhill ever since.

The Church has adamantly refused our offer of dialogue and refuses to hear what the Holy Spirit wants to say to the hierarchy through the experience of faithful Catholic gays and lesbians. A series of homophobic documents have been issued from Rome. The final most egregious document read: "The homosexual inclination, though not in itself a sin, must be considered objectively disordered." We gay and lesbian Catholics, who know that we were created homosexual by God, see this statement as a blasphemy against God by claiming that God created something that is intrinsically ordered to evil.

Now we are told that a document will be issued by Rome, using the teaching on "objective disorder," that forbids any seminary from accepting a gay candidate for priesthood, no matter how qualified, and forbids bishops from ordaining an openly acknowledged gay candidate.

This should come as no surprise. Twenty five years ago, friends in the Vatican sent me a copy of a letter sent by the Congregation of Bishops that deals with seminaries on the issue of accepting gay candidates for priesthood. At that time, the Congregation asked all seminary directors to carefully scrutinize such candidates and determine whether their homosexuality was egosyntonic or egodystonic. This psychological jargon distinguishes those who accept and are comfortable with their homosexuality over against those who see their homosexual orientation as something to be hated and rejected. Only those candidates whose homosexuality was egodystonic should be accepted as candidates for the priesthood. In other words, only the mentally sick should be accepted and the healthy should be turned away. Fortunately, most seminary directors ignored this directive. Now the Vatican intends to enforce it.

Because of the incredible success Dignity and other gay liberation groups have had over the last 39 years, very few gay candidates for the priesthood today have an egodystonic attitude of self-hatred. So the Vatican felt forced to take a more radical stance. The hierarchy has decided to scapegoat the Catholic gay community, rather than to acknowledge any failure and sinfulness on their own part.

I admire the shrewdness of the Holy Spirit. The cultic priesthood, limited to professed celibate males, whether

heterosexual or repressed homosexual, is rapidly disappearing. I can think of no action the Vatican could take
that would guarantee the total collapse of that priesthood—a
collapse that will necessarily lead to a new form of
shepherding in the Church.

In my own experience over the years, if I met a priest who
was an exceptionally good pastor, loving and compassionate,
I could be close to certain that I was dealing with a gay priest.
Let me give two examples of that. The first is my friend and
colleague, Father Mychal Judge, a gay Franciscan, who was
Chaplain to the New York City Fire Department and died
while anointing one of his beloved firefighters in the 9/11
collapse of the World Trade Towers. Mychal and I worked
together in ministry to Dignity/New York and in a special
ministry to homeless people with AIDS in Harlem. Mychal
had a deep awareness of God's love for him and felt a strong
desire to reach out and bring the message of God's love to
all those the Church and society had abandoned. Mychal
recited this morning prayer every day:

> Lord, take me where you want me to go,
> Let me meet who you want me to meet,
> Tell me what you want me to say and
> Keep me out of your way.

Mychal was a perfect model for a renewed priesthood.
His priesthood was not primarily in the sanctuary but with
the homeless in the streets or with the sick, the suffering and
the dying.

A second model of gay priesthood is Matthew Kelty, the gay Cistercian monk, until recently Guestmaster at Gethsemane Abbey and spiritual director for Thomas Merton. In his book, *Flute Solo: Reflections of a Trappist Hermit*, Matthew wrote that he attributed the special spiritual gifts that God had given him to his homosexual orientation:

> People of my kind seem often so placed, the reason, as I have worked it out, that they are more closely related to the anima (the feminine) than is usual.... Perhaps a healthy culture would enable those so gifted by God or nature (i.e. homosexuals) to realize their call and respond to it in fruitful ways.

Jesus gave us a marvelous example of how to deal with scapegoating in the story of the Gerasene Demoniac in Mark 5. The Gerasene community had picked one troubled individual and made him their scapegoat, throwing him out of town. The demoniac had accepted their judgment on him, interiorizing self-hatred, tearing off his clothes, breaking the chains that bound him, howling and gashing himself with stones. As soon as Jesus entered his presence, he became aware of God's love and that he himself was not evil but worthy of God's love and compassion. Jesus, by his love, drove out the legion of demons of self-hatred and self-destruction. These entered into a herd of pigs and their destructive evil was immediately manifested by the fact that the pigs rushed down the hillside and threw themselves off a cliff into the sea. The people of the village came out and found the former demoniac "sitting peacefully, fully clothed and in his right mind."

The people of the village became frightened because they had lost their scapegoat and begged Jesus to leave. The former demoniac asked Jesus to take him with him, but Jesus refused and instead told him: "Go home to your people and tell them all the good things the Lord has done to you. Give witness to God's love for you!" So the man went off and proceeded to spread throughout the Decapolis all that Jesus had done for them. And the people were amazed.

There is striking parallel here with us lesbian and gay Catholics. We too are being scapegoated by our Church. Many of us in the past interiorized the Church's homophobia, resulting in self-hatred and self-destructiveness. But Jesus' Spirit at one point touched our hearts and freed us from all self-rejection by giving us a clear, undeniable experience that God loves us in our gayness. Our ministry, then, like the former demoniac, is to witness to our people all the great things that God in her mercy has done for us. Our first task, then, is to call in the Holy Spirit to grant us such an overwhelming experience of God's love that we are healed of all self-hatred and self-rejection and rendered immune to the persecution of the institutional church.

We gay and lesbian Catholics must not let our enemies outside ourselves define who we are. We must let the Spirit of God, the Spirit of love dwelling in our hearts, define who we are. And then give witness to all the great things the Lord has done for us.

What, then, should be our attitude toward the institutional church? James Allison, a gay Catholic theologian, suggests that we should have the same attitude toward the institutional church as Jesus had toward the Temple: total detachment and indifference. In his ministry, the Temple was always there in the background but appears to have little relevance to Jesus' mission. As Mark noted, after the Palm Sunday procession, Jesus came into Jerusalem, entered the Temple and looked around but immediately left for Bethany with the twelve. Bethany was where the action was. Bethany was where the household of Martha and Mary, who I can imagine to be a lesbian couple and their gay brother Lazarus who was Jesus' best friend. Here was Jesus' church—a true community of love.

At the Last Supper, Jesus told his disciples that "it is necessary that I go away in order for the Spirit to come. I tell you this: unless I go away the Spirit cannot come to you. But when I go away, I will send the Spirit to you and He will dwell in your hearts and lead you into all truth." Jesus was referring to a maturing process in our spiritual life, a process for which we gay and lesbian Catholics have a special need. We must detach ourselves from all external authority and learn to discern what the Spirit has to say to us directly and immediately in our own experience.

Paul sees the coming of the Holy Spirit as the fulfillment of this prophesy of Jeremiah:

> Look, the days are coming, Yahweh declares, when
> I will make a new covenant with the House of Israel.... I
> shall plant my law, writing it in their hearts. Then I shall

be their God and they will be my people. There will be
no further need for neighbor to teach neighbor, saying
"Learn to know Yahweh." No, they will all know me, the
least to the greatest.   (Jeremiah 31:33-34)

We must fight to free ourselves from any attachment to the
institutional church, whether that be to have their approval
or the equally destructive attachment that comes from the
anger at the Church's injustice. We should see ourselves as
equals and siblings to Church authorities and pray for them
as they try to discern the Spirit of God in their lives. Leave
the Hierarchical church in God's hands. Be grateful to them
for the gifts they helped bring to us like the scriptures and
the sacraments. But do not waste one ounce of energy in
a negative attachment of anger with the Church. Commit
every ounce of our energy to the positive ministry of love to
which God has called us.

James Allison shares with us his experience of being
called by God to ministry to the gay and lesbian community.
He was on retreat in a Jesuit retreat house in Santiago in
Chile. He had been dismissed from the Dominican order for
acknowledging his gayness. The first grace he received from
God was a profound awareness that all the homophobic
violence and injustice in the Church has nothing to do
with God. This was the human Church caught into its own
blindness and sinfulness.

He was trying to discern in prayer what was God's will
for him. One day he went on a walk in a gay cruising area.
He found himself looking at some young gay men cruising
in the park and felt a strong liking for these young men and

wishing them well. When he returned to the retreat house, he went into the chapel feeling somewhat guilty for his mixed motives for going to the cruising area. He was suddenly given the grace to realize that the warm affection he felt toward the young gay men was not just his feelings but the feelings of the Holy Spirit dwelling in his heart. Then he heard a profound voice telling him: "Feed my sheep!"

He realized that that voice was God directly calling him to a ministry to lesbians and gays. That call from that moment on was an essential part of his identity, a call to priestly ministry that he could not deny or run away from without denying an essential dimension of himself. This call in no way depended on validation from the institutional church but was his direct and immediate commission from God.

Ezekiel (in Chapter 23) saw God in a vision detaching himself from the Temple in the shape of a chariot, becoming flexible and mobile. Ezekiel then had a vision of God upbraiding the shepherds of Israel (the Temple priests) for having failed to feed his sheep and abandoning them in order to pursue their own self-interests. God revealed a new understanding of shepherding, in which God Himself will undertake the shepherding. "Behold I myself will search for my sheep and will seek them out. I myself will be the shepherd of my sheep."

Judaism and Christianity are both religions of the collapsing Temple. There is always a connection between the collapse of the Temple and God bringing into existence a new form of shepherding. In Judaism, it was the collapse of the Temple in the year 587 BC which led to the creation of text-based Judaism. And, again, the collapse of the Temple in 70 AD which led to the creation of Rabbinic Judaism. In every case, the collapse is part of God's plan to get through to us and help us to get beyond something that is no longer worthy of us. It took a long time but only after Ezekiel achieved a certain form of indifference to the fate of the Temple was he able to receive the vision from God of God himself shepherding his people without any intermediary.

In the gospel of John, Jesus identifies the new Temple with his body and the body of all who have received the indwelling Spirit. Allison feels sure that anyone who has experienced God's love and has been freed from self-rejection, and then takes the final step of freeing themselves from external Church authority, will also hear the same call to ministry in their heart.

A recent example of this: a young man came to me in Fort Lauderdale. He was leading a gay life and had a lover, but he could not let go of feelings of guilt, shame and self-rejection. He was praying constantly to God to make his will known to him. As he was driving home to Boston still praying, suddenly he had a profound experience of God hugging him. This experience lasted a long time and when it was over he was sure of God's love for him as a gay man and felt a strong need to share that experience with as many as possible.

There is no doubt in my mind that we are in a new stage of the collapsing Temple and the emergence of a new form of shepherding. Joachim of Flores prophesied in the 13th century there would come a day when the hierarchical church, becoming superfluous, would in time dissolve and in its place would emerge the Church of the Holy Spirit.

Ministry in the Church of the Holy Spirit will come from the direct call of the Holy Spirit. The task of authority will be to listen prayerfully to what the Holy Spirit is saying through the people of God. This Church must become a totally democratic Church with no caste system, no higher or lower, totally equal: women with men, gays with straights, everyone possessing the Holy Spirit within them, everyone an authority.

For example, who knows what God wants from lesbians and gays? Obviously, only lesbians and gays. No one can tell us from outside what God wants of us. We are alone in knowing with an experiential knowledge that our love for each other contains the divine spirit and brings with it that kind of peace and joy that indicates the presence of the Holy Spirit.

Congratulations, Dignity/Chicago, on thirty years of faithful service to the Catholic lesbian and gay community! You have prayerfully discerned and carried out the commission the Spirit has given you. You are a foretaste of the future Church of the Holy Spirit. Continue to prayerfully discern what God is asking of you and follow that voice. Keep in mind the famous insight of Maurice Blondel: "Our God dwells within us and the only way to become one with that God is to become one with our authentic self!"

John McNeill
2 October 2005

PART 2

FESTSCHRIFT

When publication of this book was first announced Jim Mitulski, an elder in Metropolitan Community Church, and while still a graduate student at Columbia University an original member of Dignity/New York at its founding in 1972, suggested that the GLBT religious community use this occasion to publish a *festschrift* to honor the theological and spiritual contribution that John McNeill has made to the gay liberation movement.

A *festschrift* is a set of congratulatory essays made by students and disciples to a teacher, honoring him for his contribution and spelling out how his work influenced their life and work.

Several of the essays in this *Festschrift* were originally talks delivered at the opening of the McNeill-Chiarelli Archives by the Center for Lesbian and Gay Studies in Religion and Ministry at the Pacific School of Religion at the Graduate Center for Theological Studies in Berkeley, California.

Editor's Note

By
Toby Johnson

Gay Liberation is usually thought of as an extremist faction of the Sexual Revolution based in Libertarian beliefs in personal freedom, individual rights, civil liberties and equal treatment by secular government. It has been that, of course. But it has also been so much more than that. Gay Lib and the various incarnations of the homosexual rights movement are also significant and world-changing movements in religion. The issues are far more than just personal freedom; they challenge the very nature of religion and myth; they challenge the notion that religion is about saving the old and preserving tradition.

Our issues demand that all people recognize the future orientation of religion, that is, the role myth and religion should play in fostering the evolution of consciousness. The recognition of homosexuality as a character trait and personality dynamic (and not just a failing to obey moral law) forces thinking people to acknowledge both the evolution of "human nature" and, specifically, the maturation of humanity represented by psychological sophistication (with all its sex-positive implications) and awareness of the dynamics of consciousness. This recognition then forces a new—and revolutionary—understanding of the nature of God as a phenomenon of consciousness (more than as a "fact" of history). Religion, morality and mythic significance all change with context and with maturation—personal and collective.

Within the world of religion, then, the gay movement represents another of the great "heresies" that have propelled the evolution of consciousness, like the teachings of Jesus and Buddha, Galileo, Newton, Darwin and Einstein. Challenging the status quo is among *the* most religious and saintly acts.

John McNeill is one of these great "heretics" who help humanity wake up. I'm very happy to have been called upon to help produce this book with its concise and pithy statement of his life's hard fought for wisdom. Lethe Press has a mission of keeping books of gay wisdom and gay genre classics alive through state-of-the-art publishing technologies.

Offering readers this book of John McNeill's spiritual discoveries along with this series of *Festschrift* essays honoring his contribution to religion is clearly our way to joining with that contribution. Honoring John McNeill honors the evolution of consciousness that gay liberation portends.

Toby Johnson, also a former Roman Catholic religious, is author of *Gay Spirituality: Gay Identity and the Transformation of Consciousness* and *Gay Perspective: Things our [homo]sexuality tells us about the nature of God and the Universe* and four novels that convey gay spiritual wisdom. He's former editor of White Crane Journal and now an active partner in the production of Lethe Press and White Crane Books.

THREEFOLD BLESSING

BY
MARK JORDAN

Many of us hope to accomplish something during our lives that we can leave behind as a legacy. Those of us who are teachers or writers hope that we will at least once teach a class or write a book that will be remembered lovingly as a gift. Counselors, who heal by loving presence and unflinching respect, dream that their practice of the ministry of true therapy will offer chances at wholeness. And those in ordained Christian ministry—in the "priesthood," as we Catholics and recovering Catholics call it—they too hope that by preaching the Word and celebrating the sacraments, they can sanctify the earth and those who dwell on it. It is a consolation to accomplish any one of these things, but to accomplish all three is blessedness. John McNeill is blessed because he has brought this threefold blessing to so many of us.

To appreciate his blessing, remember where he stands in our history. John McNeill stands at the beginning of LGBT theology for Catholics—and not only for Catholics. He began to publish on these questions in that exhilarating moment of the late 1960s and early 1970s when it seemed as if there would be a revolution in all the major churches within the decade. I remember priests proclaiming, "In fifteen years women will be ordained. Lesbians and gays will be welcomed openly to communion. And the pope will have given away most of his power." In that giddy moment, John McNeill articulated so many of our festive hopes for the future, hopes for a personal and social transformation that would reach even into dark corners of churches. It can be hard now to remember those hopes—now when it seems that the Catholic Church has turned backwards, that women are still far from ordination and honest queer people from the communion rail, that the pope has taken even more power to himself. But after more than three decades John McNeill's message is carried as a gift in communities that are trying to imagine Christianity as something other than another human tyranny. The message of freedom from domination, the message that guides us out of the Egypt of some churches into the Promised Land where we can worship God as the queer people we are: that is the legacy in John McNeill's writings.

Remember another part of our history: the dark years during which many queer people, going to seek professional help from counselors, found angry condemnation or poisonous advice. They were told to stop being who they were in order to remain in counseling, to sacrifice the persons they loved in order to receive medical help (and what "help" they received!). If they proved resistant, they were handed over to more brutal remedies—or else to the police. In the long struggle to redeem therapy from dogmatic homophobia, John

McNeill's practice with queer people stands out because of its respectful tenderness and candid affirmation.

In third place, most powerfully for me, there is his ordained Christian ministry, his priesthood. I believe that it is an eternal priesthood according to the order of Melchizedek, a priesthood that once given can never be revoked by any merely human power. Through his ordained ministry, John McNeill has fed those around him with Jesus' meal. So many others have had to go hungry. Whenever we queer people gather in worship we are tended by the spirits of generations of believers who were prevented from coming to Jesus' table. They had to hide themselves, to mutilate themselves, as a condition of approaching Christian worship. Against that history of exclusion, John McNeill had the rare courage to be honest as a minister, to welcome all people just as he himself had been welcomed by Jesus. The spirits that cluster in churches press forward towards the table waiting for an invitation to the feast. John McNeill spoke the words to call them forward. Instead of shouting "Go away!," instead of commanding them to lie, he said, "Welcome." After so many centuries, "Welcome." Welcome to the table that is first and last Jesus' table. Welcome to the preaching of his unbounded word. Welcome to the community that is his body distributed across the whole surface of the globe for the good of all.

Let me end most personally. John McNeill had already been ordained for more than a decade by the time I converted to Roman Catholicism. As a young, passionate and very naive convert, I was deeply attracted to the Jesuits, the religious order to which John belonged. When I visited Jesuit houses, I could still glimpse something of their old system. Examinations in moral theology were once conducted in Latin, because it was essential to know how to pigeonhole the intimate sufferings brought to you in the confessional using legal Latin. You were taught that most people in hell had been hurled there for committing sexual sins. A single act of masturbation, you learned, could merit an eternity of damnation. And sex between two members of the same sex was the *crimen contra naturam,* the crime against nature, the abomination of Leviticus, the cause of God's burning rage at Sodom, and the *peccatum nefandum,* the sin that could not even be named among decent Christians. In the middle of that kind of language, John McNeill was able to teach himself new words by relying on God's loving power. He came out of that kind of bondage into liberty and integrity. He exchanged slow despair for bright confidence in God's Spirit among us. He healed himself with what I can only call a heroic holiness. Heroic holiness is how the old system defined what makes someone a saint. Why should we hesitate to draw the conclusion? John McNeill has been a saint for us.

Mark D. Jordan is R. R. Niebuhr Professor of Divinity at Harvard Divinity School. His books include *The Invention of Sodomy in Christian Theology* (1997), winner of the 1999 John Boswell Prize for lesbian and gay history, *The Silence of Sodom: Homosexuality in Modern Catholicism* (2000), a Lambda Literary Award finalist; *Telling Truths in Church: Scandal, Flesh, and Christian Speech* (2003); and *Blessing Same-Sex Unions: The Perils of Queer Romance and the Confusions of Christian Marriage* (2005).

John J. McNeill:

Jesuit Prophet, Healer, and Bodhisattva

BY

Robert E. Goss

A year after the release of *The Church and the Homosexual*, John McNeill S.J. received an order from the "Congregation for the Doctrine of the Faith," formerly the office of the Inquisition, not to make any public statements. The Vatican has never respected academic freedom and it silenced John for writing a very sensitive book about homosexuality and Christianity.

John McNeill received a doctorate from Louvain University, writing his thesis on French philosopher Maurice Blondel. He taught at Lemoyne College in Syracuse, New York, and then Fordham University. In 1972, he joined the Woodstock Theology School and Union Theological Seminary in New York City as a professor of Christian Ethics.

It was the early 1970s at the Jesuit Westin School of Theology that I would have long walks with a Jesuit friend. We had sex several times, but he was so guilt ridden and ashamed that he began an intense period of three years

of psychoanalysis (five times a week) with the Boston
Psychoanalytic Association. He was determined to rid himself
of sexual feelings and periodic slips with me. Looking back,
we were in love. But shame and guilt prevented him from
ever experiencing "making love." I started doctoral studies
at Harvard Divinity School, and he worked in a parish in
Connecticut and commuted to New York City once a week
for therapy. His therapist in New York City was Father John
McNeill. John helped my friend to learn to love himself as a
gay man, come out, join Dignity New York, and discover love
outside the Jesuits. He helped him to exchange a God of fear
and shame to a God of grace and love.

In the synagogue, Jesus recited from the scroll of Isaiah:
"The Spirit of the Lord is upon me because God has anointed
me to bring good news to the poor and to proclaim release
to the captives..." John McNeill followed in the footsteps
of Jesus not only by proclaiming release from homophobic
prisons of pathological religion but also by liberating many
folks from the closet. John helped to release my friend from
his internalized homophobia and self-hatred; my friend
was later able to discover love with another man for almost
30 years. John was a true companion of Jesus in healing
homophobia and proclaiming release to LGBT Catholics.
This is a story of grace. Grace works even when the forces of
the Vatican attempted to silence John McNeill and suppress
intelligent and compassionate theological discussion of the
tradition of homosexuality and pastoral responsibility

McNeill's *The Church and the Homosexual* was
written not merely addressed to gay men and lesbians but
to institutional Catholicism. McNeill mustered cogent

arguments from the biblical tradition, Roman Catholic natural law and moral theology, and pastoral experience of homosexuality; his contentions and line of reasoning were directed to priests, religious and church leaders. McNeill's line of reasoning had all the precision of a Jesuit philosopher—undermining traditional condemnations of homosexuality. What was revolutionary about *The Church and the Homosexual* is that McNeill's gave careful attention to the biblical texts often erroneously applied to homosexuality. There were direct influences from Jesuit biblical scholars at Woodstock Theology School in New York and from a young gay historian—John Boswell at Yale University. John Boswell and John McNeill were active in Dignity.

McNeill's book—translated into numerous languages— was moderate from our perspectives of contemporary queer theology, yet it was as revolutionary in its time as any queer theology in the last decade. It turned moral arguments upon themselves from the findings of psychology, scripture, and moral theology. McNeill made the case for a new pastoral approach to the condition of homosexuality. He did not accept the judgments of earlier Catholic moral theologians that those gays/lesbians unable to change their sexual orientation had to live a life of forced abstinence.

Later John McNeill would note that those gays/ lesbians choosing celibacy did so for unhealthy reasons. In the meantime, he noted that celibacy might be ideal but was pastorally unrealistic for many gays/lesbians. Taking a more pastorally realistic and a more compassionate approach, McNeill allowed for responsible, ethical same-sex relationships.

184 ROBERT E. GOSS

One year after its publication, the Congregation for the Doctrine of the Faith found McNeill's book contradicting Catholic moral teaching on homosexuality. The Vatican Congregation under the Prefecture of Cardinal Franjo Seper could not tolerate a softening of Catholic teaching or a compassionate response to homosexuality. Its duty was to safeguard Catholic moral doctrine from the highly questionable approach of John McNeill. The Vatican ordered that the *imprimi potest* (approval from the Jesuit Provincial that the book was suitable for public presentation and discussion) be removed from the book and that John McNeill be prohibited from public discussion: (McNeill: 1993, 223-231) "It seems urgent that Father McNeill be prohibited from any further appearance or lecture on the question of homosexuality and sexuality, or in promotion of the book." (McNeill: 1993, 230) The Congregation ordered John McNeill to remain silent in the media on the issue of homosexuality. This meant an end to interviews, public appearances, professional lectures and public writing on homosexuality.

As a good Jesuit under the vow of obedience, John McNeill observed the imposed silence for nine years. For awhile, John had been in training to become a psychotherapist from Institutes of Religion and Health in New York City. He used his training in psychology, pastoral counseling, and spiritual direction to pursue a private ministry to Catholic gays/lesbians through Dignity, a psychotherapeutic practice, workshops, and retreats. During those years, John helped to release many gay/lesbian Catholics from the burdens of internalized homophobia and ecclesial homohatred. Many folks—including my Jesuit priest friend—moved from guilt, shame, social ostracism and ecclesial stigma into healthy self-images, relationships and to integrate their sexuality and spirituality.

On Halloween 1986, Cardinal Joseph Ratzinger released the infamous letter on homosexuality: Letter on the Pastoral Care of Homosexual Persons. There was nothing pastoral about the letter that described gays/lesbians as "intrinsically evil" and "objectively disordered." Ratzinger's letter ignored all scientific evidence on the biological and psychological basis of homosexuality and disregarded all contemporary biblical exegesis applied to homosexuality. It was violent, mean-spirited and aggressive, intending to curb Dignity, pastoral sensitivity to gay and lesbian Catholics and deny scientific trend towards a more open and tolerant society in the United States. When I read Ratzinger's letter, I wondered about its rhetorical urgency. I was sure that it was immersed in the closeted dynamics of the gay Catholic priesthood. (Jordan: 2002; Goss and Boisvert: 2005) But the letter's irrationality, vehemence, and scapegoating made me wonder why Cardinal Ratzinger was so obsessed with this particular issue. I found such internalized self-hated in closeted homosexuals. The current purge of the Catholic seminaries of gay men by Pope Benedict XVI now leave me no doubts of his projection of his own self-struggles onto the LGBT community.

John McNeill spoke out against Cardinal Ratzinger's letter to the US bishops. This set in motion a process of his expulsion from the Society of Jesus. Ratzinger ordered John to cease all ministries to gays and lesbians. Unlike the Dominican Order that rallied to the defense of Edward Schillebeeckx when he was under investigation of the Congregation for the Doctrine of Faith, the Jesuit hierarchy caved into the pressures from Cardinal Ratzinger. John Paul II had broken the independent theological and intellectual spirit of the Jesuits in the 1980s; and there were few Jesuits outside John's own community that stood up against his unjust dismissal. John had been a member of the Jesuit order for 40 years; the Jesuits were his family. Without any benefit of social security or royalties from his book, John was expelled from the Jesuits.

The noted biblical scholar Walter Wink wrote John McNeill about his expulsion:

> John, when the Vatican imprudently slammed the door on you, the gust of wind it set off blew open hundreds of doors. In the craftiness of God, I swear your impact will be increased exponentially. (McNeill: 1993, 241)

Wink's prophetic words were realized in John McNeill's subsequent writings. *Taking a Chance on God* moved him in the direction of delineating pathological religion. McNeill brought his philosophical background in Maurice Blondel, Thomist theology, and his practice as a psychotherapist to delineate the nature of pathological religion. He makes explicit his indebtedness to Blondel's philosophy of freedom in his appendix in the third volume of his trilogy. (McNeill: 1995, 195-204) Blondel's notion of radical immanence grounds his theology of human developmental maturity, authority and freedom. It plays a philosophical role here and in his third volume.

McNeill first starts from the premise that good theology is grounded in good psychology. Grace and nature are intimately intertwined. Years of his counseling practice and retreats with gay men and lesbians provided him with the insights for his second book where he delineates pathological religion as based on fear, shame, guilt, and self-hatred. He first hand experienced the institutional dysfunction of Roman Catholicism and saw its ravages in the lives of his gay and lesbian clients. There is no question that in his discussion of pathological religion, McNeill has in mind institutional Catholicism. However, he directs his second book to gays/ lesbians, their lovers and families, and friends to speak of sexual orientation and gender identity as blessing from God. He notes, "Positive gay pride is pride in our sense of hospitality and compassion." (McNeill: 1996, 98) Hospitality and compassion are prominent virtues in the LGBT community. McNeill breaks restrictive Catholic theology of sexuality by discussing "sex as play." For him, LGBT sex as it matures in healthy patterns can restore to Christian theology an understanding of sexuality as joyful, playful, and mystical gift. Such theological insights escape from Church teaching and certainly disturb Catholic hierarchs' understanding of human sexuality.

The message in McNeill's second volume and further expanded in the third volume of his trilogy is that the homophobic Roman Catholic Church offers teaching that harms directly the psycho-spiritual development of LGBT folks. LGBT Catholics need to look to other means of spiritual validation of our original blessedness. LGBT Catholics need to look to the Holy Spirit rather than to Church authorities— to speak to our direct experience to discover our blessedness and lovableness in the eyes of God. LGBT Catholics find out what God wants for their lives through the "discernment of spirits."

But what caught my attention in his second book written at the height of the AIDS pandemic in the gay community was McNeill's appropriation of the spirituality of the Buddhist Bodhisattva vow of compassion:

> I take upon myself the burden of my suffering brothers (and sisters), I am resolved to do so, I will endure it, I will not turn or run away, I will not turn back. I cannot.
>
> And why? My endeavors do not merely aim at my own deliverance. I must help all my brothers (and sisters) cross the stream of this life which is so difficult to cross. With the help of compassion I must help them across the stream.
>
> I would fain become a soother of all sorrows of my brothers (and sisters). May I be a balm to those who are sick, their healer and servant until sickness come never again. May I become an unfailing store for my poor brothers (and sisters) and serve them in their need. May I be in the famine of the ages end their drink and meat.
>
> My own being, all my life, all my spirituality in the past, present, and future I surrender that my brothers (and sisters) may win through to their end, for they dwell in my spirit. (McNeill: 1996, 104-105)

As a doctoral student in Indo-Tibetan Buddhism at Harvard, I wrote my first graduate paper on how the Jesuit ideal of "finding God in all things" and the Bodhisattva path overlapped. I sat in the presence of a Bodhisattva in 1979 when Tenzin Gyatso, the Fourteenth Dalai Lama, came to

Harvard and met with the four students learning classical Tibetan. The Dalai Lama exuded such compassionate presence and mindfulness that he radiated love and peacefulness. That year I took the Bodhisattva vow of compassionate. It was congruence with the Christ of the gospels whose compassion led him to the throw-away people of his society. The Bodhisattva vow was at the heart of Jesuit spirituality, the core of the Spiritual Exercises of Ignatius of Loyola.

John McNeill's life now radiated the spirit of the Bodhisattva vow, and he rightly mirrored Christ's own attitude—that of compassion. He articulates a genuine spirituality of gay and lesbian Christian in a positive way. *Taking a Chance on God* was one the first positive Christian books on gay/lesbian spirituality. The importance of the concept of the Bodhisattva is revisited in final volume of the trilogy and his autobiography. It grounds his discussion of compassionate identification with the suffering LGBT community. (McNeill: 1995, 39-50)

McNeill's third volume—*Freedom, Glorious Freedom*—breaks out as his most queer book. LGBT folks cannot adhere to the teachings of homophobic religious leaders. John McNeill succinctly writes about the central them of his book:

> When we gays and lesbians discover that we cannot follow the fallible teachings of our religious authorities without destroying ourselves, then we are forced to search out what God is saying to us through our experience and take personal responsibility for choices that we make. I believe that the Holy Spirit is using the fallibility of the religious authorities to guide the Christian community

into a new level of maturity and responsibility necessary for spiritual growth of the human community in today's world. (McNeill: 1995, 11)

John McNeill introduces the reader to the rules of discernment of St. Ignatius of Loyola after the previous chapter's exploration of freedom of conscience and LGBT maturity. McNeill gives numerous case histories for discerning God's Spirit in gay/lesbian lives, but what was even more powerful was the narration of his own personal discernment on whether he could in conscience abandon ministry to gays and lesbians when his Jesuit superiors under pressure from Cardinal Ratzinger ordered him to stop ministering to gays and lesbians.

> ....I so much want the truth of Christ's life to be the truth of my own that I find myself, moved by grace, with a love and desire for poverty in order to be with the poor Christ; a love and a desire for insults in order to be closer to Christ in his own rejection by people; a love and a desire to be considered worthless and a fool for Christ, rather than to be esteemed as wise and prudent according to the standards of the world. By grace, I find myself so moved to follow Jesus Christ in the most intimate possible, that his experiences are reflected in my own. In that, I find my delight. (McNeill: 1995, 42)

Here we enter into the interior prayer life of John McNeill; we catch a glimpse into his courage to stand up for the truth that God was indeed calling him to hold institutional Catholicism accountable for its pathological practices which harmed the emotional, psycho-spiritual integration of sexuality and spirituality of LGBT folks. Nearly sixty-one years old, John made a retreat at the Trappist monastery at Gethsemani to discern whether he would accept the Vatican's ultimatum to completely abandon his LGBT ministry, psycho-therapeutic practice, and remain silent as an obedient Jesuit. Gethsemani was the monastery of the famous Trappist writer and contemplative Thomas Merton who began a serious dialogue between Christian and Buddhist monastics. A Trappist monk gave John McNeill a copy of the Bodhisattva vow.

The Bodhisattva embodies compassion for the suffering, and he/she embraces exile until all beings are saved: "I take on the burdens of my brothers (and sisters)…" (McNeill, 1995, 43) McNeill took the Bodhisattva vow and he understood right away its connection to his prayer during his retreat many years ago making the Spiritual Exercises and asking for the "Third Degree of Humility" in imitating Christ's life. It was a decision between compassionate suffering and solidarity with the LGBT community or caving into the Vatican and Jesuit bureaucracy. It was a choice to follow the movement of the Holy Spirit in grace rather than the pathological religion of the Vatican and his Jesuit superiors. Both *Freedom, Glorious Freedom* and his autobiography *Both Feet Firmly Planted in Midair* elaborate on the painful process and his finding joy in his discernment process to obey and follow Christ over the Vatican and his Jesuit superiors.

John McNeill chose God's grace over the comfort of religious order that had been his family for forty years; he had not pension or medical insurance. He was stripped of his priesthood and publicly humiliated by the Vatican and

church leaders. Without a safety net, John stepped in out
in faith at age sixty-one for the truth of God's compassion
and love for the LGBT community. He chose the spiritual
maturity of freedom to be Christ's disciple, abandoning
institutional pathology and dysfunction of the Roman
Catholic Church. What is significant in his last volume is
his personal testimony of discerning God's authority and
will, not in homophobic church teachings, the abandonment
of his ministry to LGBT Catholics, and compliant silence.
He understands well and prefigures the later LGBT rule of
discernment popularized by ACT UP: Silence = Death. He
exemplifies the process of discernment that he calls upon
LGBT Catholic to embark upon, to enter a Catholic exile, and
find God in their personal experience and prayer lives and
not in the Catholic authority.

After many years, I had the opportunity to finally meet
John McNeill and his lover Charlie. I went to Washington DC
in November 2000 to join Soulforce to protest the National
Conference of Catholic Bishops convened in a yearly meeting.
Soulforce was protesting the hateful teachings of the Roman
Catholic hierarchy.

I was already a transferred priest to MCC and now a
part-time clergy on staff with MCC of Greater St. Louis and
full time professor of Comparative Religion. I traveled to
Washington D.C. to join Soulforce's protest of the National
Conference of Bishops. My personal agenda was not
Soulforce's agenda; my agenda was very personal to my own
transition from a Jesuit priest to MCC clergy. I had gone to
put an end to my unresolved feelings about being a Catholic
priest in exile, my angers at the many Catholic priest friends

who died of AIDS, and my outrage at clerical sexual abuse scandal and the complicity of Catholic priests to shelter priests and child molesters. Part of my resolution took place in an early after breakfast meeting in the lobby of the hotel and the holding cell of the D.C. Police when later arrested.

I had an early breakfast and journeyed to the lobby to await transportation to the National Catholic Basilica where the Soulforce was staging it protest and arrest action. I sat down on sofa next to John McNeill. We began to talk as former Jesuit priests, still living the vision of Jesuit spirituality. It was two former Jesuit theologians engaged in conversation. But I became a disciple at the feet of an experienced healer. I sat at the feet of a great Jesuit Bodhisattva, a person committed to a life of compassion and justice for the LGBT community. John was the second Bodhisattva that I met. He had the same compassionate mindfulness and peacefulness of the Dalai Lama. He had been a hero through his life and books. I told John about a book review that I had published of *Freedom, Glorious Freedom* and how I understood his journey as praying for the Third Degree of Humility during the Spiritual Exercises of Ignatius. I thought John McNeill was truly a Catholic Bodhisattva, a prophet and a healer.

Later that day, we challenged a major human prison—the Roman Catholic Church. Countless LGBT (and other folks) have experienced the institutional ravages of shame, guilt, fear, and exclusion. We got arrested together at the Catholic Basilica: John with his lover Charlie, and I with a 72 year-old heterosexual woman from Ohio. We followed Jesus into the homophobic temple of U.S. Roman Catholicism and ACTED UP, and we were arrested.

Let me end with my endorsement quote on the back cover of his autobiography *Both Feet Firmly Planted in Midair*:

> John McNeill is one of my heroes. He will be remembered as the gay saint of the twentieth century who initiated a Catholic Stonewall while the Church in fear tried to closet him and to expel him because he believed that Christianity is fundamentally about kindness and inclusion.

Robert E. Goss, Th.D. has been Pastor/Theologian of MCC in the Valley since June 2004. Goss received his doctorate from Harvard University in Theology and Comparative Religions with a specialization in Indo-Tibetan Buddhism and Christianity. He is a former Catholic Jesuit priest who left and transferred his credentials into MCC as clergy. He is the author of *Jesus ACTED UP: A Gay and Lesbian Manifesto* (1993), coeditor of *A Rainbow of Religious Diversity* (1996), *Our Families, Our Values: Snapshots of Queer Kinship* (1997); *Take Back the Word: A Queer Reading of the Bible* (2000); and *Queering Christ: Beyond Jesus ACTED UP* (2002). He is co-author of *Dead But, Not Lost: Grief Narratives in Religious Traditions* (2005) and coeditor of *Gay Catholic Priests and Clerical Sexual Misconduct: Breaking the Silence of Sodom* (2006). He is Co-editor of *The Queer Bible Commentary* (2006).

For five years, Goss has served as co-chair of the Gay Men's Issues in Religion Group of the American Academy of Religion. He served on the National Advisory Board of the Center for Lesbian and Gay Studies in Religion and Ministry of the Pacific School of Religion (Berkeley, CA). Goss has been involved in a number of peace and justice movements from ACT UP and Queer Nation in the early 1990s.

John McNeill, Pastor

BY
Jim Mitulski

There are many things that we're proud of today—the Graduate Theological Union and the reception of the McNeill Archives by the Center for Lesbian and Gay Studies in Religion and Ministry. But, as a Pacific School of Religion graduate, I must take the opportunity to brag on my school: it was PSR that had the courage and the foresight to establish CLGS, the first center of its kind in any seminary in the world, and it was CLGS that has brought the McNeill archives here today. And let me acknowledge publicly Pacific School of Religion as the coolest seminary in the GTU.

It is a great honor to be here tonight as part of the celebration and I want to take a moment and just ask that if you're a Catholic here, by your own definition—that means perhaps you were baptized in the church, perhaps you were confirmed in the church, perhaps you no longer go—but you know what I mean when I say, "You're a Catholic." Would you, the Catholics here, stand for just a moment? Let's give ourselves a hand for being here, for being alive.

I say that because John McNeill means something to us who are Catholics that is even more profound than you who are Protestant will ever know. It's the part that makes me feel somewhat emotional even as we gather here. There's something about being a Catholic: it's a contradiction you live with your whole life long, and it's also something that you'd love to be as proud of as you are proud of being GLBT.

I remember at the beginning of *Portrait of the Artist*, James Joyce's character describes to a friend saying, "I've lost my faith," and his friend says, "Have you become a Protestant?" He says, "No! I said I had lost my faith, not my reason."

Catholic is who you are, not just what you believe. It's not just another denomination. And, John, you are the pastor to the Catholics in the church and to the vast number of Catholics who for reasons of self-respect, dignity and a deep relationship with God have left the church. But you're our pastor and that's what I want to lift up tonight.

I'm going to give a personal testimony about how important John's work has been to me and to my own work as a pastor. *The Church and the Homosexual* came just at the right time for me in the mid-70s. My mother is a graduate of a Jesuit university; and when I was 18 and coming out to her, to be able to hand her this book, written by a Jesuit—not a Benedictine or a Franciscan or a member of one of those other orders. Hey, you know that I'm telling the truth—the Jesuits are the Cadillac of Catholic religious orders. Published by a Jesuit priest with an *imprimi potest*. OK, it's not an *imprimatur*, but it's almost as good.

There was nothing like it because she understood and the Catholic hierarchy understood (and every Catholic who picked up this book understood) that what it was saying, couched carefully but plainly, was this: it's OK to be gay. Now I gave this book to my mother back in 1976 when I came out to her and I remember when I came out to her that the first words out of her mouth were, "Are you a homosexual?" And I said, "Yes." And she said, "Then remember that God made you and that God loves you unconditionally and never let anyone tell you differently—not even the Church." She's the product of a Jesuit upbringing—what can I say?

And I remember that a few weeks later I was talking to her on the phone (I was then back in New York), and she was crying and saying that she was glad that we'd had this conversation and she said, "You know, I'm glad we talked, but I just wish that you could change." That was a little hurtful for a moment; I thought we'd had a little regression at that point. And she said, "No, I don't mean about being gay. I wish you could be Catholic." And that's really the core issue for many people—gay people and non-gay people: we have been told that we cannot be Catholic even though it was our birthright, even though it is the religion of our ancestors, even though it is who we are our whole lives long. And, John, with this book and your subsequent life and ministry you have restored something that cannot be taken from us: you have reminded us that we always have a place.

These archives are important and will prove to be important to religious scholarship because of what John has done, not only in terms of GLBT scholarship but there are other items that belong to the archives that scholars will find important. It's important also to GLBT scholarship because John says it first plainly and clearly like few others did and still do. It's important to GLBT religious scholarship, too, because eventually, when the history of this period is written, we will come to understand that it was religious people and the conflicts that took place in the church that often guided what happened around the issue of GLBT rights in secular society—it's not just a church issue, but it's also about our place in society; and, as it goes in the church, so too it goes in society. And, John, you have provided guidance not only in the church but in society for your work.

But, most importantly, I think that John's work is important to GLBT Catholics because he is our pastor and he has made sure that even though the church abandoned us, we were not left alone. John McNeill is a scholar, an activist, and a pastor to the churched and the post-churched.

I want to remind us of the church of the 1970s into which this book appeared. This is pre-John Paul II. It was during the ascendance of liberation theology; some parishes were being run by councils and pastoral teams composed equally of priests and nuns in many places. These were experiments that were so successful that they had to be killed. Everybody knew that married priests were just about to happen and women priests were not far beyond that. Divorced people were hopeful that their new marriages would be recognized shortly and in many parishes they received communion openly. Many priests openly counseled the use of birth control. Communion was given in the hand for the first time—communion in both kinds. There were female altar servers, or, as they called them in my parish, "girl altar boys." No wonder we turned out the way we did! And Catholics were even singing like Protestants. That's the context. It was a time of great optimism that the church would be different, that it really would be what Vatican II had dreamed about. This is the context in which John made these three simple assertions to scholars and also to people outside the church.

One, is that homosexuality is not contrary to but is supportive of the will of God. Two, is that homosexuality is part of God's plan and that homosexuals, gay people—we didn't use the word "gay" that much then—have a unique role to play in God's creation. And his third thesis, which was perhaps the most exciting one, is that love and sexuality in the context of gay relationships can be a way of coming closer to God. These were the things that got John in trouble for when he said them.

And he made this important connection in *The Church and the Homosexual* that I also want to lift up to us because I think that it's become even clearer as the church has become more conservative again:

"The church's attitude toward homosexuals is another example of societal injustice equally based in questionable interpretation of scripture, prejudice and blind adherence to merely human traditions—traditions which have been falsely interpreted as the law of nature and of God. In fact, as we have seen, it is the same age-old tradition of male control, domination and oppression of women which underlies the oppression of the homosexual."

This was a brilliant insight even before its time that has become even more true as we've seen how the church has revealed its truly patriarchal nature.

John, you taught us through your work and through your witness to think independently; you taught us to listen to our consciences and to believe independently. To keep changing and growing. Every year I always looked forward to what it was that you would talk about at Kirkridge [Retreat Center in Pennsylvania] because I knew that there was no issue you were afraid to grow toward or engage with. You've gone a lot of different places and you've been very candid not only in the religious press but in the secular gay press about sexuality. What a great model for a priest and for a pastor!

You taught us that sometimes it's OK to say "no," and sometimes it's OK to speak up. Sometimes we have to act up, act out, and not let anyone else define us. You taught us that we can serve God in the church or we can serve God outside the church. You taught us not only how to be free, but how to free ourselves because we were part of that Catholic self-reinforcing world. It's almost like a cult—and I say that cautiously, but if you grew up in it you know what I'm talking about. The one thing you can't ever do is challenge it. It teaches you from the earliest moment to be fearful of claiming your own authority. And, John, you taught us to claim our own authority as a spiritual act.

This is what it was like to hear John McNeill in the mid-1970s. I was there as a member of Dignity New York then, like a lot of good Catholic boys—that's mostly who went there. We were the parochial school graduates, all moved to New York City, trying to figure out what it meant to be gay. We were obedient unto death; and we met, like Christians in the catacombs, on Saturday nights in apartments all over the New York City for Dignity masses because no church would have us. You had to come one Saturday to find out where the next Saturday's mass would be.

Now the people who cared for us, we who were Puerto Rican and Italian and Polish and Irish and German boys, were the Jesuits on 98th Street and a nun named Sister Mary Lou Steele. They were our pastors, and we met in these houses on Saturday nights, and they taught us to love ourselves and to free ourselves, and we couldn't do it on our own. We needed priests and nuns to set us free, and they did—not to cultivate our dependence on them, but to learn to be strong, self-sufficient, spiritual and sexual people. Once a month we had a big gathering at Good Shepherd Faith Presbyterian Church on 66th Street (again, in a Presbyterian church because the Catholic Church wouldn't have us). We would hear the Jesuits come and talk to us in a big group about the issues of homosexuality and spirituality.

There were people there in that room who have gone on to do things important to our movement—Joe Kramer, who founded the Body Electric School, and Andy Humm, who became a great gay/lesbian rights activist. Many of John's therapy clients were there, unnamed of course, but, John, you know how many people you helped set free through your therapy practice. I was there.

We've all left the church and yet we've reinvented it in the best tradition of Vatican II, in the spirit of Jesuit scholarship, in the spirit of Martin Luther, in the spirit of Jesus— "You shall know the truth, and the truth shall set you free." You taught us to claim our own authority, you taught us that good science is good theology and that God gives us intellect and spirit and, because of the religious world view in which we had been raised, we needed someone to show us a different way. We needed a pastor. You were, and are, our pastor—the good pastor that the church didn't provide for us.

There's a passage of scripture in John 10 that reminds me of John McNeill. Just so you Protestants know, we Catholics do know the Bible; we don't always choose to use it, but we do know it. Listen to these words from the Gospel of John and think about John McNeill's life and ministry.

> I am the Good Shepherd. The Good Shepherd lays down his life for the sheep. The hired hand who is not the shepherd and does not own the sheep sees the wolf coming and leaves the sheep and runs away, and the wolf snatches them and scatters them. The hired hand runs away because the hired hand does not care for the sheep. I am the Good Shepherd. I know my own, and my own know me, just as God knows me and I know God. And I lay down my life for the sheep. I have other sheep that do not belong to this fold; I must bring them also and they will listen to my voice so there will be one flock, one shepherd.

John, you were not afraid to lay down your life, your career, your ministry, your credentials for the sheep—the people that you were called to pastor. And we heard your voice and we knew that it was true.

I remember the first time I heard John speak in the basement of that Presbyterian Church: it was packed, wall to wall. This is not usually how homosexuals spend their Saturday nights in New York City, and this was really true in New York in the 70s. Trust me—I was there. We gathered in that basement of that Presbyterian Church to hear you speak, and you talked about your devotion to the Virgin Mary, you talked of our special gift to take care of our families. Sometimes when you talked we rebelled, we snickered. We didn't want to hear about the Virgin Mary and how we were there to take care of our parents. We were drawn to it, and we were put off by it too. And yet WE HUNG ON EVERY WORD THAT YOU SAID. And this was one of the most dramatic moments I remember from your speaking in that basement of that Presbyterian church when you told the story that you recount in your autobiography (*Both Feet Planted Firmly in Midair*) of your conversion, of your decision to become a priest, when you were a prisoner of war in a concentration camp in Europe and starving, just starving, and you depicted for us in vivid terms what it felt to be starving.

You said that a Polish peasant tossed you a crumb, or a crust of bread, or a potato—yes, it was a potato—he tossed you a potato at great personal risk to himself, knowing that if anyone saw him tossing you that food he could be shot and killed, and some were for doing that very thing. He tossed you a potato and wordlessly made the sign of the cross, and you said in that moment you knew that you were called to be a priest.

This is an image I have of John McNeill. I don't want to trivialize or demean or in any way misrepresent by falsely comparing the plight of gay people to the plight of people in prisoner-of-war camps, but there was a definite emotional and spiritual connection we made as you described what it meant to have your face pressed against a fence, and then having someone at great personal risk toss you a potato to nourish you and making the sign of the cross.

That's what you did for us, John, and that's what you taught us to do for others. To risk our lives even, and our careers and our ministries, in order to bring sustenance and nourishment to those who are desperate for it and who could only do it because people took risks.

Many times when I was a pastor during the AIDS years, Catholic parents especially would have the worst time because they would be there with their children, with their sons, who were dying, and they would say to me through their tears, "Why does the church make me choose between me and my son? Why does the church tell me I shouldn't be here when my son is dying?" And I thought of what I learned from you, John, and I realized that I only had one task in that situation—to help set these Catholics free, to respect where they were but to go right to where they were in their situations and help set them free.

This is why you were our pastor, John, because you were not afraid to do what needed to be done because you taught us to set ourselves free.

Some day, when seekers and scholars want to examine how the church changed from what it is right now to what I know it will become as a result of your work, they will come here to the GTU to study at the McNeill archives. And they're going to have an experience reading through your work, reading through all the correspondence around it, and the testimonies that result, and seeing what came as a result of it. They're going to be proud to be gay, and they're going to be proud to be Catholic. And their minds will be opened, and they will dedicate themselves also to the work that you stand for—setting yourself and others free. Thank you, John.

Rev. Elder Jim Mitulski has pastored within the gay affirming Metropolitan Community Church since 1983 and was appointed Elder serving the denomination's Region 2 in November 2005. At present he is pastor of the MCC church in Berkeley, California.

Jim has served MCC congregations in New York, San Francisco, Guerneville and Glendale. His 15 year service as Pastor of MCC San Francisco coincided with the height of the HIV health crisis. By the time he left that congregation in 2001 he had officiated at over 500 funerals, sometimes 6 to 8 a week. Immediately prior to his appointment as an Elder, he served on the staff of the denomination's West Hollywood headquarters, being responsible for leadership development and seminary relations.

His education includes a BA in religion form Columbia University, an M.Div, from Pacific School of Religion; he was a Merrill Fellow at the Harvard Divinity School. In 2002 he was awarded an honorary Doctor of Sacred Theology from the Starr King School for the Ministry. He completed the coursework for a doctorate in Ministry from the San Francisco Theological Seminary. He is currently enrolled in the D. Min. program at the Episcopal Divinity School in Cambridge, MA.

He is a trustee at Pacific School of Religion and serves on the national board of the Center for Lesbian and Gay Studies in Religion and Ministry.

Rev. Mitulski has authored chapters on issues of Queer Theology and Aids activism in books such as: *Out in the Castro: Desire, Promise, Activism; Take Back the Word; The Church With AIDS.*

HOLIER THAN THOU:

JOHN J. MCNEILL'S CONTRIBUTION TO THEOLOGY AND MINISTRY

BY

MARY ELIZABETH HUNT

I am honored to join my friend and colleague John McNeill on this historic occasion when the Pacific School of Religion and the Graduate Theological Union receive a spiritual and intellectual treasure more precious than gold. It is always a pleasure to be with John and his life partner, Charlie Chiarelli, because they embody the best of what John writes.

As a GTU alum, I am proud that our institution, which, thanks to the Center for Lesbian and Gay Studies in Religion and Ministry, with the creative leadership of Mary Ann Tolbert and Bernard Schlager, is in the forefront of a new theological sub-specialty. I congratulate you on this accomplishment and encourage you to continue *ad multos annos*, as John McNeill's beloved Jesuits would have it.

I am pleased to join Jeannine Gramick, whose ministry has been effective enough to have her silenced, and Jim Mitulski, whose ministry I have admired for many years. It is great to have "a good Irish Catholic boy" like Jim Donahue with us. Jim and I go back to our graduate school years here on Holy Hill. His presence as a representative of the wider theological community is proof of what I will outline, namely, that John McNeill has had an enormous impact on theology and ministry, indeed on GLBTQ theo-politics, within and beyond Catholicism.

I have entitled my remarks: "Holier Than Thou: John J. McNeill's Contribution to Theology and Ministry," because I think it is important to contextualize and claim John's work as part of the contemporary Catholic scene. I do this both for purposes of scholarly rigor, because that is where John's work is rooted, and for purposes of redemption, that it might help to undo some of the virulent "homohatred" and duplicity for which the Catholic Church is responsible.

Today's event is a delicious irony in light of John's history with the institutional, or what Elisabeth Schüssler Fiorenza has so helpfully called the "kyriarchal," Catholic Church. He was silenced by the Congregation for the Doctrine of the Faith shortly after the publication of *The Church and the Homosexual* in the late 1970s, and forbidden from speaking in the public arena on these matters, though he continued his private psychotherapy work.

In 1988, he was ordered by Cardinal Ratzinger to cease all ministry with the GLBTQ community, an order he chose not to obey. As a result, the Jesuits caved in to Vatican pressure to expel him from the Society of Jesus.

I predict that, long after most of us are dead, scholars will come to this archive to read John's side of the story. They will discover what we already know, that John is "more Catholic than thou" and that he was correct when he claimed that being gay and Catholic were not mutually exclusive. They will rehabilitate his reputation and probably name a Jesuit university after him (perhaps University of San Francisco will become John McNeill University!). I see no reason to wait, as the data are now or soon to be catalogued, accessible, and online. Happily, we can begin the process today.

My theory is that the Jesuit order was so full of gay men that they realized John could not comply with the Vatican's directive to cease ministry with gays except by leaving the Society. Simply by celebrating mass with his brothers he would be in violation! But I will leave that speculation for another day and note simply, as John would, that the Holy Spirit always has the final word. In this case, indeed she did.

The Roman silencing of John McNeill by unlawful decree resulted in profound intellectual and spiritual sounds: the completion of John's trilogy (*The Church and the Homosexual, Taking a Chance on God* and *Freedom, Glorious Freedom*); a fruitful ministry as a therapist that led many people from guilt and shame to ease and pride about their sexuality; hundreds of lectures and workshops around the world; more than two decades of retreats at Kirkridge, a conference center in Bangor, Pennsylvania, where every year a remarkable community gathers to be "Gay, Lesbian, Bisexual and Christian"; generous nurture of the Catholic lesbian and gay group Dignity after co-founding the New York City chapter; citation in virtually every subsequent book in the field as the Catholic pioneer; honors and awards from secular as well as religious groups; not to mention being named Grand Marshal of the New York City Gay Rights

Parade (1987); all distilled with spiritual maturity in his autobiography, *With Both Feet Firmly Planted in Midair*. Because of John's work, many people began to realize that being Catholic and queer was not a contradiction in terms, but a joyous reality.

In light of John's remarkably productive life, I am tempted to ask Cardinal Ratzinger if he might silence me just a little! But indeed, the irony gives way to deep regret when I imagine how much more of an impact John McNeill might have had if the Catholic Church had instead lifted up his brilliant intellectual and spiritual insights. Imagine if the Jesuits had been courageous enough to stand up to Rome and affirm John's prophetic claim that just as psychologists learned that homosexuality per se is not pathological, theologians have no choice in conscience but to reconceptualize our approaches as well. The work could have begun earlier and been woven into catechesis and documents as one day it will be when the Catholic Church admits its errors on homosexuality as with Galileo on science. Thanks to John, we began the work, and continue it through the steady theological production on these questions that this Center was founded to promote. How fortunate we are to have John's original materials at hand.

Happily, the Center for Lesbian and Gay Studies in Religion and Ministry is engaged in inter-religious and international work. But let me highlight how John's work is Catholic as an example of how one's tradition shapes one's contribution to the whole. The Catholic community claims to be unique in that it is "one, holy, catholic and apostolic." These attributes have led to ecumenical stalemates, but I think in the case of

John McNeill they form the most appropriate framework for assessing his work because they encompass the fullness of his project.

Dr. McNeill's approach is "one" insofar as he intends and achieves, in my judgment, an intellectual and spiritual integrity. John's life was not a straight line to sainthood; indeed, some would say there was little straight about it! Rather, his good Upstate New York Irish values (which I share) and his experience as a prisoner of war resulted in a Jesuit who strove for honesty, who knew suffering up close.

Mark Jordan, in his marvelous book, *The Silence of Sodom,* describes Catholic ecclesial culture as so fraught with lies and deceptions that I can see how John McNeill must have been very confused by what he saw up close and personal as a priest. I understand why he ultimately chose to reject membership that conferred clerical privilege in favor of a deeper "oneness." His own integrity and that of the Gospel on which the whole religion was allegedly based trumped his desire to belong to the Society of Jesus. Sad. Nonetheless, the Jesuits' loss was the whole church's gain as he extended his ministry to the Metropolitan Community Church, and, indeed, to all who seek him.

On to holiness. Frankly, I have always felt slightly uncomfortable around people who are said to be holy, because the word is so vexed and the reality so powerful. But there is a "holiness" to John McNeill that I trust. Throughout John's writing, and more so in his being, I always sense a deep connection with something most of us only hope to glimpse. I admire his reliance on the Eucharist and prayer, habits he shared with his sister, a nun, who prayed daily for GLBTQ people in her cloister until her death. For me, the most telling mark of holiness is John's amazing love for the Church despite unjust treatment by its officials. Likewise, his enduring love for the Jesuits despite their collective inability to be brothers is transparent. This kind of holiness impresses me.

"Catholic" takes on new meaning in light of John McNeill's work. It is not simply the axiomatic "small c" equals "universal" approach. Rather, catholic, thanks to John McNeill, now means concerned with the whole truth, with the whole world, with the full meaning. Contrast this with the myopic world of *imprimaturs, nihil obstats* and pedophilia cover-ups. This is why John McNeill is respected in the wider gay community as a gay Catholic priest because he is one, despite it all. I take John's approach and consider myself Catholic, thanks, and urge others to do the same. Another small irony: Rather than being judged as heretics, I predict the many GLBTQ Catholics who seek to change the kyriarchal profile on this matter will one day be seen as apologists.

The "apostolic" nature of his work is his firm conviction that theology is done in service of people, not people in service of theology as those who traffic in mandatums would have it. Rather, John's writing, from his study of Maurice Blondel to his most popular articles, is always geared to the needs of people who struggle to be faithful.

And his pastoral ministry, much of it private and unsung, is that of a steady Irish priest who knows human failings and rejoices in human diversity. His writings provide other pastoral ministers with the tools to do the same. This is no small contribution.

These four dimensions of John McNeill's work—one, holy, catholic, and apostolic—leave the Catholic Church as a whole in his debt. They also account for his enormous popularity, I might say iconic status, among GLBTQ Catholics and our friends. But his impact goes well beyond his roots to persons of diverse faith perspectives who seek to hold together their sexuality with their faith. If a Roman Catholic priest can do it and be open and proud about it, why not a devout Muslim, a Southern Presbyterian, or an Orthodox Jew? As our collective movement matures, his example becomes more obvious.

John McNeill has had the good sense not to presume to speak for women. I would not want to overstate the case and call him a feminist. But his experiences of being treated as a second class citizen in his own church dovetail with those of his feminist sisters who seek equality and dignity in the same circles. Among us he is loved as an ally and welcomed as a brother. Surely his notion that one could be gay and Catholic spilled over to those of us who are lesbian and Catholic. We remain in his debt as we work out the implications for ourselves, delighted to have his accompaniment though our paths may sometimes go in slightly different directions. We know that he is listening to women, like his dear sister, and praying for change.

John and I disagreed once quite publicly at a Kirkridge conference on the matter of death. I had delivered myself of a long-winded oration stressing a feminist approach to death, suggesting that it was not so much an individual matter but a common one. Following Rosemary Radford Ruether, I affirmed that we will all be part of the great matrix, the compost if you will, from which new life will spring. John was my respondent. He fairly bounded to the podium to protest in a classically Catholic priestly manner, stressing individual immortality. He assured the audience that when he dies he is confident he will run into the arms of his loving Father who will call him "Little Jackie McNeill" for all eternity. As you can imagine, the contrast between our views was vivid! Happily, neither of us knows yet who was right, and I pray we won't find out for many years to come. Moreover, I suspect in hindsight that we both may be surprised. That is the fun of theology done with trusted colleagues.

That John and I, two Irish Catholics from Upstate New York, can share so unselfconsciously the insights of our theological imaginations, disagree at points, and still welcome one another at the table of blessing is what matters. This is what it means to be "more Catholic than thou." Thanks to John McNeill, it is possible and I am grateful. I only hope the model spreads to the world's billion Catholics that we in turn might learn to live peacefully with far more profound differences among our neighbors.

Mary E. Hunt, Ph.D., is a feminist theologian, co-founder and co-director of the Women's Alliance for Theology, Ethics and Ritual (WATER) in Silver Spring, MD. A Roman Catholic active in the women-church movement, she lectures and writes on theology and ethics with particular attention to liberation issues. She is author of *Fierce Tenderness: A Feminist Theology of Friendship* (Crossroad, 1991); editor of *A Guide for Women in Religion: Making Your Way from A to Z* (Palgrave, 2004) and co-editor, with Patricia Beattie Jung and Radhika Balakrishnan, of *Good Sex: Feminist Perspectives from the World's Religions* (Rutgers U Press, 2001).

John McNeill, Prophet

BY
Sister Jeannine Gramick

As a founder of the New York chapter of Dignity, the organization for lesbian and gay Catholics, John has smoothed the way for Dignity members to maintain respect for the institutional Church while at the same time confronting its inadequacies.

ENERGIZING

The prophet energizes the community to fresh forms of faithfulness, vitality, and hope in God. John's 1988 book *Taking a Chance on God* called lesbian and gay Christians to replace a God-relationship based on fear with one based on love. John's lifelong struggle to accept his own gayness as a gift of God encouraged his readers to overcome interiorized homophobia, shame, guilt, and fear engendered by religious and societal prejudice. His works have enabled thousands to grow into a spirituality based on love and giftedness

His 1995 book *Freedom, Glorious Freedom* rejuvenated lesbian and gay Christians. It encouraged them to follow their conscience and thus to reconcile their faith and trust in God's love and mercy with their own self-acceptance. It helped those who have known the secrecy and fear of the closet to experience the liberation of the Holy Spirit.

John has energized lesbian and gay Christians to give personal witness to the Church about the holiness of their lives and their love by means of his own personal witness of fidelity and love with Charlie, his lifetime partner. John has enabled them to grow into a deep and joyous relationship with God through the retreats he conducted for more than 20 years at Kirkridge, an ecumenical retreat center in the Pocono Mountains of Pennsylvania. He continues to facilitate retreats called "Intimacy with God for Gay Men."

AMAZEMENT

The prophet can be described only with the language of amazement. And this is the language we use when we speak of John McNeill.

We are truly amazed by John McNeill, priest, therapist, theologian, teacher, author, advocate for gay and lesbian liberation and man of prayer.

We are amazed by his uncommon courage to walk down the lonely road of ecclesiastical censure so that others may amble down the freedom trail of self-acceptance and a legitimate following of one's conscience.

We are amazed by his willingness to assume the daring task of questioning the sexual ethic defended by an authoritarian institution at the risk of professional sacrifice, personal security, assaults on his good name and dismissal from his Jesuit community.

We are amazed by his lifetime of dedication and service to the spiritual and moral development of gay and lesbian Christians in the face of stigma and rejection.

We are amazed by this instrument of God's compassion who has helped millions of lesbian and gay men to see themselves as expressions of God's deep and generous love.

John, we salute you as a prophet for our times and acknowledge our debt of gratitude for the witness of your life.

Jeannine Gramick (born 1942) is a Roman Catholic nun, and a co-founder of the activist organization New Ways Ministry.

Gramick has written and edited numerous articles and books. Her books include *Homosexuality and the Catholic Church*, *Homosexuality in the Priesthood and Religious Life*, *The Vatican and Homosexuality*, *Building Bridges: Gay and Lesbian Reality and the Catholic Church*, and *Voices of Hope: A Collection of Positive Catholic Writings on Lesbian/Gay Issues*. *Building Bridges* was translated into Italian and published as *Anime Gay: Gli omosessuali e la Chiesa cattolica*.

Gramick is the subject of a documentary film *In Good Conscience: Sister Jeannine Gramick's Journey of Faith*, by the Peabody and Emmy award-winning director, Barbara Rick.

TEACHER AND FELLOW JESUIT

BY
VINCENT VIROM COPPOLA

John was both my teacher, when he was a Scholastic and I was in prep school, and later a fellow Jesuit in the Society, when both of us were studying Philosophy, he finishing off his degree in Paris and me just beginning the love of wisdom in the Philosophate. So we go back a few moons.

When I had him in prep school, his classes were always exciting and filled with discussion. I recall one in particular when he asked if Joseph Stalin could be killed by an individual for the greater good of the world? Without realizing it we were arguing Bonhoeffer in our fourth year English class. These many years later I am still arguing ethics and trying to ground a universal and purely human ethic, and I think I might have John to blame. A couple of years ago, when he was in the hospital with pneumonia, I sent him my book *Quest: A Search For A Soul For Modernkind, A Book On Being Human*. I received such a wonderful response from him. Today, I use his book in my religious ethics class to open up the students to a 21st Century approach to homosexuality. John suffered to stay true to the honest and honorable stand

he took. He was abandoned by his Jesuit superiors, who forgot
or really didn't want to know who the Jesus they took their
name from was. They never challenged, if I might say with
a touch of bitter irony, the Pope of pious legalism, who like
the Grand Inquisitor in Dostoevsky's novel forgot or really
didn't want to know who Christ was. John chose love over the
law and didn't forget and really lived Christ-consciousness.
Because of the crucifixion that followed because of his stand,
he rightfully becomes an exemplar for the gay as well as the
entire truly Christ-conscious community. How ironic that he
was expelled from the Jesuits for acting like Jesus.

I had long since left those Renaissance halls for the coast
and California, and for a long period of time lost contact
with John, and certainly with the nonsense being spouted
out of the mouths of the Church leaders. Unfortunately,
such nonsense has not abated. What has changed, however,
and due in part to John's journey, is the way gay people
look upon themselves and Christ. In one of his books he
mentions among so many other liberating things, the story
of Jesus and the Centurion, and how the gender-specific
word in Greek used in the gospels brings home to the honest
reader with even a minimal historical sense that this was
the Centurion's lover. Jesus goes to the home of the man
and ministers unto the lover and tells everyone that there
is no greater faith in all of Palestine than this Centurion's.
At communion, I believe Catholics still use the Centurion's
words, "Lord, I am not worthy that you should enter under
my roof." Of course, the Vatican might have changed that
with all the homophobia coming out of the place. *Vecchia
fama nel mondo li chaima orbi!* No matter about them, John's

books live on. I should mention here that he also shows the different kind of family that Lazarus, Martha, and Mary had, all whom Jesus loved—how applicable to today. John became a true companion of Jesus by embracing love, which is really the only measuring rod, not only for any companion of Jesus, but for the spirituality of any human being. Camus was so right in calling rebellion a strange form of love. John McNeill was and is a lover.

He who abides in love abides in God, and God in him.

Vincent Virom Coppola teaches philosophy, theology, and cinema in three different departments at CSUN, California State University Northridge. He has four degrees, two advanced degrees in philosophy, one advanced degree in fine arts, and an AB in literature. He is a member of the Writers Guild of America and Broadcast Music Incorporated. In filmmaking, he has gone the full spectrum, from concept to composite, doing preproduction, production, and postproduction. This included acting as producer, director, or writer among other things. He has also worked in theater, where he also produced, directed, and wrote. Finally, he has written a philosophical book called Quest, and is working on another.

HOMOSEXUAL HOLINESS
THE COURAGE OF JOHN J. MCNEILL

BY
VIRGINIA RAMEY MOLLENKOTT

During the several decades I worked with John McNeill at the Kirkridge Retreat Center, I often heard him emphasize the fundamental principle that bad psychology leads to bad theology. Naturally, this essential insight shows up in his books and articles, for instance, "unless we are dealing with a sadistic God, what is destructive psychologically for so many people has to be bad theology!." (*Freedom, Glorious Freedom*, p.46) And conversely, "Whatever is good psychology is good theology... we are called by God to choose life." (*Taking a Chance on God*, p.29) Being a New York psychotherapist working with hundreds of gay clients, and having a background of Jesuit training and ordination to the priesthood, perfectly equipped John McNeill to become the first public spokesperson for, and defender of, gay and lesbian people in the Roman Catholic church. So authentic has been McNeill's Catholic ministry that it has achieved universality, helping Protestants like me and people of other religions and no religion, gay or non-gay in their journey toward wholeness.

McNeill's psychological insights are impossible to separate from his spiritual and theological counsel. Delighting in Bernard of Clairvaux's famous assertion that "Everyone has to drink from their own well," McNeill wisely warned that many of our cultures messages to gay people are polluted by homophobia, so that it is necessary to learn the discipline called discerning the spirits. This in turn involves listening to our own hearts and trusting our first-hand experience: only in this way does our own well become safe for drinking. In this connection, McNeill encouraged Catholics to be thankful that God has created Roman Catholic authorities fallible and imperfect—because these weaknesses stimulate the development of adult freedom of conscience.

Keenly aware that gay and lesbian young people constitute 30% of all youth suicides in the United States, McNeill never failed to point out that self-hatred is nothing less than sinful. He likes to quote Henri Nouwen's observation that "Self-rejection is the greatest enemy of the spiritual life because it contradicts the sacred voice that calls us the "beloved." His careful distinction between the ego as defined by psychology and ego as defined by classic spirituality bridges McNeill's parallel vocations.. Psychologically speaking, we human beings must develop an authentic, strong conscious self, called ego; spiritually speaking, we must turn away from the prideful ego that refuses to acknowledge its dependence on other people and its divine source. But self-rejection is deadly to others as well as to oneself. As McNeill has observed, "Those gay men most likely to act out their sexual needs in an unsafe, compulsive way... are precisely those persons who have internalized the self-hatred that their religions impose on them." (*The Church and the Homosexual*, 4th ed. p. xv)

As psychotherapist McNeill stresses the importance of basic trust, acknowledging that because of his mother's death when he was only four years old, he has had to struggle all his life to re-establish trust and hope in he universe. (Because of early incest, I have been forced to engage in a similar struggle—which may be why McNeill once said he found it easier to work with me than many other lesbians he had met). At the same time he taught his hundreds of clients and thousands of readers, students and retreatants that our ultimate trust must be lodged in God's love, because we cannot expect any limited human lover to be our God, who meets all our needs. (Perhaps this attitude explains how Jack and Charlie have been able to remain loving partners for well over four decades.)

It takes huge patience to work with an institution as tremendous and intransigent as the Roman Catholic Church, and McNeill quotes Vaclav Havel to the effect that "Hope... is not the conviction that something will turn out well, but the certainty that something makes sense regardless of how it turns out." Such an attitude is essential for peace-with justice activists in any cause or tradition. Otherwise advocates are soon burned out by the sluggish pace of progress and the unpredictability of results.

Through the years I have witnessed John McNeill's growing awareness of language, because of the way language controls the world view of entire cultures. As a feminist and trans-activist, I have appreciate his contempt for binary gender stereotypes and the social programming that perpetuates them. Above all, I appreciated his emphasis on the fact that in order to have intimacy with God, we must be intimate with our own deepest self, as opposed to submitting to a power external to ourselves. For this reason, "coming out" is not only a developmental phase but a spiritual journey toward experiencing God's indwelling Spirit. "The process of lifting the burden of guilt, shame and low self-esteem for a lesbian or gay person (or bisexual or transperson) is identical to the process of "coming out." (*Taking a Chance on God*, p.67) Underneath all that guilt and shame we discover spiritedness, aliveness, joy. We discover holiness.

For more than two decades I worked as a co-presenter with John McNeill at Kirkridge's annual four day retreat for lesbians and gay Christians. Minutes before my first presentation at my first of these retreats, I panicked, thinking that someone may ask me about one-night stands, something I had never experienced. John's advice: "Virginia, never put down anybody's attempt to relate." In his fourth edition of *The Church and the Homosexual*, John expands on this advice, explaining that many people are incapable of entering into a monogamous faithful relationship, which he called "the human ideal." Having learned from his extensive psychotherapy career that "the vast majority of people living out a life of abstinence do so for pathological reasons." (*Freedom*, p.204), he advises "all gay people to develop the most intimate relationship possible for them." (Freedom, p.205)

I remember my pleasure when John did a cute little dance to the tune of "Taking a Chance on Love" after one of his Kirkridge presentations. I also remember my awe at learning that John met with retreatants who signed up for 15 minutes private conversations during free times on Friday and Saturday afternoons, often tuning around lives during those few but highly charged moments. Once I worked up the courage to offer my time in a similar way, I was astonished at how much meaningful growth can occur in a mere 15 minutes when people arrive prepared and clear about their intention.

I was impressed with John's enthusiasm abut the twelve step programs (Alcoholics Anonymous and its many offshoots) which he calls "the most powerful spiritual liberation force in the world today." (*Freedom*, p.93). Because I had so often heard John praise the twelve steps and refer to all addictions as forms of idolatry, when I realized that I was addicted to relationships, I found it natural to seek out an Al-Anon group near my home. I never found it necessary to admit that my problem was not an alcoholic partner but instead a workaholic partner, because the principles were the same for either. I feel sure that the help I received from Al-Anon (and indirectly from John) has been replicated in many hundreds of lives.

From the first time I attended John's Kirkridge retreat I sensed that the participants were very mature spiritually. I might have been intimidated had I known then what I know now; that the vast majority of the men were priests attending under assumed names. Being with them and the wonderful lesbian women I met did more than any amount of theorizing to empower me to leave my closet behind.

I was the third wheel at the time Mary Hunt and John McNeill locked horns about personal immortality. Mary felt hat the desire to retain one's bodily identity after death is somewhat pathological, agreeing with Rosemary Ruether that unlike men, women can be satisfied with being subsumed into a great matrix from which new life arises. My position in this three way debate was experience based: as I have identified more and more with the Spirit of God within me, I have become more fully myself, not less myself; so I assume that eternal life will include a glorious individual identity that is currently beyond my wildest imagination. But I vividly remember John's dance steps as he proclaimed his faith that in eternity he will forever be known as "Jackie McNeill."

I am in awe of the courage John has shown by speaking the truth to the vast power of the Vatican. He has dared to announce that any gay person who follows the "moral" advice of the Church and the religious right will end up destroying their own mental health and spiritual maturity. He has asserted that the primary teacher in the Church is not the hierarchy; it is the Holy Spirit, and the Spirit dwells in our hearts and speaks to us through our own experience. (*Freedom*, p.105) He has even dared to assert, regarding the Centurion of Luke 7 and Acts 10 that " at every communion rite in the Roman Catholic Church the last words that a communicant says before receiving holy communion are 'Lord I am not worthy to receive you, but only say the word and I shall be healed.'" McNeill comments, "I believe that God has a divine sense of humor and moved a Church prone to homophobia to use the faith confession of a gay man every time we receive the Lord in the Eucharist." (*Freedom*, p.136)

This kind of courage carries with it a steep price. For John McNeill the cost was being expelled from the Jesuit order, his home and his family for forty years, losing his old age pension and health insurance, being deprived of the right to exercise his priestly calling and being attacked publicly by the Vatican. I also remember John's frequently describing his sorrow at losing the right to be buried in the Jesuit graveyard at Auriesville, New York. He now plans to have his ashes scattered in the memorial garden at Kirkridge in Bangor, Pennsylvania, where a plaque will make known his final words to the world:

Here lies a Gay Priest

He took a Chance on God!

And truly since his birth in 1925, the life of John J. McNeill has been a courageous life of homosexual holiness.

Virginia Ramey Mollenkott taught English language and literature at the college and graduate levels for 44 years after earning her B.A. at fundamentalist Bob Jones University, her M.A. at Temple University and her Ph.D. at New York University. She served as a stylistic consultant for the New International Version of the Bible and served on the National Council of Churches committee to prepare an Inclusive Language Lectionary.

She is the author, editor and co-author of hundreds of articles and twelve books, including *Women, Men and the Bible* (1977, revised 1988), *Is the Homosexual My Neighbor: A Positive Christian Response* (1978, revised 1994), *The Divine Feminine: Biblical Images of God as Female* (1983), *Sensuous Spirituality* (1992, revised and expanded, 2008), *Omnigender: A Trans-Religious Approach* (2001, revised and updated, 2007), and *Transgender Journeys* (2003) She has one son, three granddaughters and a delightful partner named Judith Suzannah Tilton.

"You saved my life."

By
Mel White

An open letter to John McNeill

Dear John,
    I suppose you've heard these words countless times but I need to say them again: "You saved my life." And though that claim might seem a bit hyperbolic, something of great and lasting importance happened to me while reading your book, *The Church and the Homosexual*.

I remember almost exactly when it happened. In 1976, I was well on my way to a complete nervous breakdown. For about 23 years I had struggled to keep in check my desperate need for same-sex intimacy. The passion to love one of my own kind came rushing to the surface when I was just 13 at the 1953 Boy Scout Jamboree in Irvine, California. When all the other boys were talking about their girl friends I was hiding my half-crazed crush on Darrell, my tent mate at the Jamboree. It was my first infatuation and the object of this totally unexpected and unexplained obsession was a boy and not a girl. From that confusing, gut wrenching moment my life was filled with secret torment and constant fear with a lot of guilt thrown in (and I'm not even a Catholic).

The Church and the Homosexual was published in 1976. At the time besides being a husband of a wonderful woman and the father of two great kids, I was writing books and articles, making documentary films, co-pastoring with my wife, Lyla, a Covenant Church in Pasadena, California, teaching communications and preaching at Fuller Seminary, and traveling on speaking tours across the US like a whirling dervish hoping that I could accomplish enough "good deeds" that God would forgive what had become by then my almost overwhelming yet unfulfilled need to hold and be held by another man. (In those days I knew as little about God's amazing grace as I did about homosexual orientation.)

I had been counseled by a string of Christian therapists who promised me that if I would just read the Bible and meditate regularly enough, pray hard enough, fast long enough, and take showers cold enough that God would "take away this temptation" and set me on the straight and narrow road to health and happiness. After going through two failed exorcisms to "cast out the demon of homosexuality" (one in a Catholic monastery the other with a devout charismatic friend), I begged a behavioral psychologist at Fuller Theological Seminary to use electric shock to "treat my illness." He frowned but didn't try to dissuade me from this desperate measure and finally under pressure gave way.

I can still remember the young psych grad student who wired me up. I had been instructed to bring to the session pictures of handsome young men and beautiful young women. The pictures were shuffled and placed before me. The treatment was simple. When the assistant turned over a photo of a handsome young man, I was to push the button that would release enough electric current to shock me. But when the photo of a beautiful young woman came up, I could release the button and end the shock. Needless to say, it didn't work and the ultimate irony is that while going through this ridiculous process I was feeling definite attraction to the handsome young man holding the cards.

On September 20, 1976, Presidential candidate Jimmy Carter stood on his porch in Plains, Georgia, while being interviewed by a reporter from Playboy magazine and admitted for the record that "I've committed adultery in my heart many times. This is something that God recognizes I will do—and have done—and God forgives me for it." Playboy readers may have laughed at Mr. Carter that day, but just hearing a man of his standing (and a Baptist at that) talk openly about his own sexual struggle gave me hope.

Of course in those days I was still thinking that my homosexual thoughts were simply "committing adultery in my heart." I had no idea that in fact my homosexual orientation was also a gift from God to be accepted, celebrated and lived with integrity. That brand new idea was given birth in my heart and mind by your book, *The Church and the Homosexual*.

In 1977, while pastoring a congregation in Pasadena, I discovered a study commissioned by the Catholic Theological Society of America entitled *Human Sexuality: New Directions in American Catholic Thought*. In the dim light of a dusty used bookstore in Glendale, California, I scanned the index, skipped past the chapters on marital and pre-marital sex and turned to pages 186-219, the chapter labeled "Homosexuality." I was happily surprised by what I read there.

For decades I had scanned dozens of theological and psychological books by Evangelical Christian authors warning that the destruction of Sodom was a clear example of God's wrath on homosexuality and homosexuals and that for centuries practicing homosexuals had been called Sodomites as a kind of warning of the certain consequences of their sins. But on page 193 of New Directions in Catholic Thought I read this sentence: "There is not the least reason to believe, as a matter of historical fact or of revealed truth, that the city of Sodom and its neighbors were destroyed because of their homosexual practices." And the footnote that sourced this shocking conclusion said simply, "See J. McNeill, *The Church and the Homosexual*, pp. 42-50."

Needless to say I found your book that day and turned immediately to pages 42-50. In those few pages you made it clear that societal prejudice and unexamined ancient tradition had lead to a complete misunderstanding of the Genesis account of the destruction of Sodom. You supported your premise that Sodom's destruction came from the city's inhospitality to strangers in your own translations of the Hebrew text and on D.S.Bailey's ground breaking 1955 book *Homosexuality and the Western Tradition*.

Introducing me to the writings of D.S.Bailey was another of your special gifts to me. Now I understand why Bailey and McNeill were not quoted by the Evangelical authors I had read who misused a handful of verses to condemn homosexuality. Bailey's careful and courageous translations of the Old and New Testament verses we call the "clobber passages" led to the decriminalizing of homosexuality by England's Parliament in 1957 and your book *The Church and the Homosexual* led to the eventual emancipation of gay and lesbian Christians like myself who had spent whole lifetimes as victims of Evangelical and Roman Catholic authors who misused Holy Scripture to support ancient prejudice and modern intolerance.

Reading your book I learned that the biblical reasons given for the fiery destruction of Sodom could be found in the writings of five Hebrew prophets and in a sermon by Jesus himself. All those miserable, self-hating years I was lead to believe that Sodom was destroyed by God's wrath against men having sex with men. Then you quoted Ezekiel's words to the contrary: "Behold, she and her daughters lived in pride, plenty, and thoughtless ease; they supported not the poor and needy; they grew haughty and committed abomination before me; so I swept them away, as you have seen." (Ezekiel 16:49-50)

But in *The Church and the Homosexual* you also dared to take on the Greek Testament passages used to condemn homosexuals. In footnote 160 of that Catholic study, *Human Sexuality,* the author's used your exegesis of I Cor. 6:9 to help clarify the ancient misunderstanding of the text: "McNeill argues that the *malakoi* and *arsenokoitai* in the first instance with 'soft' dissolute behavior in general and in the second instance with male prostitution."

While turning the pages of your *The Church and the Homosexual*, I experienced the first real glimmer of hope that maybe, just maybe religious leaders were wrong when they declared homosexuality "a sickness to be healed and a sin to be forgiven." And though you made a strong psychological case that homosexuality was just another of God's mysterious gifts, I was most impressed that you were finding your evidence as a theologian and biblical scholar in the very same Book that so many churchmen were using to caricature and condemn me.

Although I had heard rumors about the personal price you paid for writing *The Church and the Homosexual*, I didn't understand the details until 1995 when I read your *Freedom Glorious Freedom: The Spiritual Journey to the Fullness of Life for Gays, Lesbians, and Everybody Else*. Once again, one of your books was perfectly timed to help see me through a difficult period in my own life as a gay Christian. My autobiography, *Stranger at the Gate: To be Gay and Christian in America*, had just been released. My life had been profiled on 60 Minutes, Larry King Live and on other television and radio programs and in newspapers and news magazines across the US.

As a result, my former Evangelical clients dumped me. My publishers wouldn't even consider the proposals I sent their way. My once best selling books were taken off the shelves of Christian bookstores and my once prize-winning films disappeared almost overnight from the film libraries of the members of the Christian Film Distributors Association who had twice honored me as filmmaker of the year. I was no longer welcome at either of my *alma maters*, Fuller Theological Seminary where I taught for 14 years after earning my masters and doctorate there or Warner Pacific College where I served on the board of trustees whose members voted unanimously to grant me an honorary doctorate "for my valuable contributions to the church and to the nation."

And I think the saddest surprise was realizing that I had become an untouchable to most of my Evangelical friends including hundreds of students I had taught at Fuller and hundreds of parishioners I had pastored at the Covenant Church in Pasadena, California.

During my own rapid slide from hero to outcast I read your *Freedom Glorious Freedom* and found that in 1977, shortly after the release of *The Church and the Homosexual*, you had been "ordered to silence" by the Vatican on the issue of homosexuality. Taking seriously your vow of obedience to the Society of Jesus and the Vatican, you obeyed giving up your writing, your teaching and your preaching ministries. My own losses were nothing in comparison to the loss of freedom you endured for the next eight years of silence.

Then, in 1985, after a keynote address on the freedom of conscience at a National Dignity Convention, an organization of LGBT Catholics that you helped found, you were ordered to "withdraw from any and all ministry to homosexual persons" by Cardinal Ratzinger (now Pope Benedict XVI but then head of the Congregation for the Defense of the Faith, previously called the Holy Inquisition.) I could only imagine the pain you suffered when you were ordered to abandon your mission to the extent you couldn't even be associated in any way with gay causes "including passive attendance at a meeting or liturgy."

It's no wonder that this new order by the second most powerful man in Christendom caused you to seek out guidance from those you trusted most. It was the advice given you by a former Jesuit Provincial and your spiritual guide that set bells ringing in my heart. You wrote, "I described to him all the pros and cons I had been debating, he suggested that I was going about the discernment process all wrong. I was too much in my head. He told me that if he went outside his apartment in the South Bronx and saw someone lying at the curb, and asked what was wrong, and was told he or she had no food and no bed to sleep in, then he knew what God was asking of him—to find food and shelter for this poor human being."

At that time, so many of my sisters and brothers were suffering outrageous forms of intolerance and discrimination. I hadn't really experienced that suffering until I joined and been ordained by the Metropolitan Community Church, a network of more than 300 congregations across the US made up primarily of lesbian, gay, bisexual and transgender Christians no longer welcome in the churches of their childhood. Gary and I moved to Dallas, Texas, after being called to serve as Dean of the Cathedral of Hope, with roughly 2,000 members serving at least another 10,000 LGBT people in the greater Dallas area. We had moved from the comfort and safety of gay-friendly Laguna Beach, California, to a large city where we experienced firsthand the suffering of our sisters and brothers.

I conducted my first funeral in nearby Tyler, Texas, where a young Baptist who sang in his local church choir had been kidnapped, tortured, and shot countless times before dying naked and alone in a gravel pit just miles from his home. His killers thought they were doing the country a favor by eliminating another queer. It was becoming more and more obvious to Gary and me that the evangelical leaders for whom I had ghost written their autobiographies were poisoning the national discourse about homosexuality and homosexuals with their antigay campaign on radio and television, in their magazines, newsletters and fundraising campaigns. And the consequences were tragic in the lives of the LGBT people Gary and I had been called to serve.

Something had to be done to end this rhetoric of intolerance. In that spirit, Gary and I and a handful of friends staged a lonely fast-for-understanding at Dobson's headquarters in Colorado Springs. During that seven day fast, there were so many threatening calls that the local police asked us to move into a hotel from our trailer in the shadow of the Focus on the Family international operations center.

That same year, after being arrested while protesting Pat Robertson's antigay tirades on his 700 Club telecasts, I was visited in jail by Lynn Cothren, a gay Christian activist who earned his living as Coretta Scott King's personal assistant. He had flown from Atlanta with Mrs. King's blessing and had brought me a copy of her husband's *Why We Can't Wait*. During that first visit Lynn introduced me to the principles of *Satyagraha*, truth force or better known by both King and Gandhi as Soulforce. These principles of relentless nonviolent resistance became the foundation for Soulforce, the organization Gary and I founded in 1998 to protest and hopefully help end the religion based oppression of our LGBT sisters and brothers across North America.

My son, Mike, once said to me, "If you hadn't been gay, Dad, you would never have known what it feels like to be an outcast." He was so right. In your *Freedom Glorious Freedom*, another of my heroes, Walter Wink, theologian and biblical scholar, wrote you these words. They are so descriptive of exactly what has happened to me.

"John, when the Vatican imprudently slammed the door on you, the gust of wind it set off blew open hundreds of doors. In the craftiness of God, I swear, your impact will be increased exponentially."

Amen and amen! John, you've written so many helpful books, letters, speeches, sermons and articles since then that helped move me and thousands of others from self hatred to self acceptance and spiritual renewal. In 2000 the people of Soulforce gave you our Heroes Award for a lifetime of heroic labor on our behalf. That same day you stood vigil with more than a hundred volunteers from Soulforce and Dignity at the US Conference of Catholic Bishops, protesting once again their false teachings about homosexuality and the tragic consequences of those teachings. As the bishops passed through our vigil line, they were handed an open letter you had written. I've attached a copy of that open letter. (Editor's Note: The open letter appears in this volume as the Appendix on page 153.) It is as clear and as prophetic now, eight years later as it was in 2000. Thank you, John, for your courage and your commitment. We are grateful.

For thirty-five years, the Rev. Dr. Mel White struggled to "overcome" his homosexual orientation through prayer, fasting, various aversive therapies, exorcism, and even electric shock. A victim of misinformation and biblical misuse, Mel thought his same-sex orientation was a sickness and a sin. During those "closet years" Mel served the Christian church as a prize-winning television producer and filmmaker, a best-selling author, a pastor, seminary professor, and ghost writer to religious leaders including Billy Graham, Pat Robertson, and Jerry Falwell.

After a time of terrible depression, Mel finally reconciled his Christian faith and his sexual orientation. In his autobiography, *Stranger at the Gate: To Be Gay And Christian In America*, Mel announced, "I'm gay. I'm proud. And God loves me without reservation."

Mel and his partner, Gary Nixon, have traveled across the country as the UFMCC Minister of Justice seeking equality and understanding for God's lesbian, gay, bisexual and transgendered children. In 1997, Mel and Gary received the ACLU's National Civil Liberties Award in Atlanta, Georgia, for their efforts at applying the "soul force" principles of Gandhi and King to the struggle for justice for sexual minorities.

Satan or Saint?
Let History Decide

By
Daniel Helminak

On October 8, 1976, Catholic theologian John Giles Milhaven published a review of *The Church and the Homosexual* in *National Catholic Reporter*. That was the first I had heard of John McNeill, its author, and hope sprang anew in me.

By that time, at age 33 and already ordained a Catholic priest for eight years, I was finally grappling with the realization that I am homosexual, and my conscience was not at peace. Periodically, destructive qualms of self-doubt and guilt—"Maybe you're just fooling yourself. The devil is leading you astray"—continued to rack my soul. I was too sincere in my religious commitments—indeed, in my more basic commitment to sheer honesty—to be able to blow off the doubts. My logical and reasonable mind and my personal integrity demanded more certainty.

A beginning answer came from John McNeill's book and set me on my own life's journey of thought, study, writing, and teaching about sexuality and spirituality. I read John's book and had to agree with Milhaven. No conclusion had been irrefutably proved, but the evidence John laid out certainly raised serious doubt about the official Catholic teaching on homosexuality. That all homosexual acts were inherently sinful was now questionable. Major new evidence was surfacing. Recent biblical exegesis and social-science research did not support the traditional condemnation.

According to Catholic teaching, questionable moral obligations should not be imposed on people. No one can be required to bear a moral burden that might not really be necessary. (At heart, Catholicism is actually a deeply compassionate religion.) This principle is so standard that it even carries a Latin tag: *Lex dubia non obligat*: A doubtful law has no binding power. On this principle alone, the question of homosexuality should have already been settled. While biblical scholars, social scientists, historians, and Vatican officials continued to explore the matter, individual believers should have been given the freedom to pursue their own best counsel—had the Vatican only been true to ordinary Catholic teaching.

Of course, matters are seldom so simple. Power structures do not bend easily. Not only did the Vatican not loosen its chains on the souls of lesbian and gay people; over ensuing years, the Vatican intensified its efforts to suppress all gay liberation. And not only the Vatican—other traditions maneuvered similarly. The Baptist principle of "soul freedom"—that every believer may interpret the Bible as seems appropriate in his or her own life—also went by the board. And solemn endorsements of historical-critical interpretation of the Scriptures across the traditions got bracketed when same-sex behavior was in question.

In the big picture, these responses are understandable. The approval of same-sex relationships shakes the foundations of Western civilization. Even apart from sexual matters, social change has become assaultive: easy mobility, frequent relocation, Internet communication, culture wars and terrorist threats, religious violence, changing gender roles, mushrooming pluralism and diversity, philosophical uncertainty about knowledge itself, economic and cultural globalization. Our world is changing precipitously. The human psyche is not made to sustain such rapid-fire change. So the churches' reluctance to voluntarily adjust long-standing ethical teaching is hardly surprising.

Still, I wonder how much better our world and religions would be if our leaders were only honest. Couldn't the Vatican have simply acknowledged that new information had raised doubts but that the seriousness of the issue called for caution and prudence? Couldn't the issue have been at least opened up for discussion? Couldn't a long-term communal learning process have been inaugurated? Other churches have taken this tack. Of course, they are suffering their own disruption over attempts to study and adjust sexual ethics. But is the harm caused there less or more than that caused by the Vatican's stonewalling? Would the task of the other churches be easier if the *über* powerful Vatican took an honest stance? At least the honest approach lets our "yes mean yes, and our no mean no," as Jesus recommended (Matthew 5:37). And an honest approach takes the unfair burden off of individuals while the collectivities rethink their stance.

At this moment in history, to read the first lines of Milhaven's review provokes irony, if not heartbreak: "The system works!" he boldly stated. "It worked halting and sputtering. But the book is now in print with the official permission for publication of McNeill's Jesuit superior."

Yes, in those days many of us actually believed that the Vatican would change its teaching. Optimistically, we thought that the system would work. Evidence would prevail. Truth would win out. The church would change. There was hope that Vatican Council II would, indeed, open a window and let fresh air into the church, as good Pope John XXIII had intended. But then—after the mysterious and premature death of Pope John Paul I—there began in 1978 the creepingly suffocating, almost interminable pontificate of John Paul II. Bit by bit he tightened the screws, and the Catholic hierarchy once again represented a lock-step army of loyalists. Rather than concern for the good of the people and the future of a budding global community, power and insidious control strangled the life-hope of the Catholic Church.

Given the evidence on sexual orientation that has accumulated since McNeill's groundbreaking book, it is astounding that the Vatican continues unbudgingly to insist on its myopic position. Today, not just reasonable doubt about a traditional teaching, but the overwhelming bulk of the evidence in every field of study weighs against the Vatican teaching. Understood in its own historical and cultural setting, the Bible is indifferent to same-sex relationships. Biopsychosocially, homosexuality is a normal variation. Same-sex relationships can be as life-giving as any heterosexual love—or when misused, just as destructive as misused heterosexuality. The evidence could hardly be more convincing. In difficult matters such as these, such compelling clarity is seldom achieved. Nothing but absolute incompetence or diabolical dishonesty could explain the persistent negativity of Vatican teaching.

Yes, "the system works." But it appears to work best for the Vatican, not for the benefit of everyday Catholics and others throughout the world who are unavoidably influenced by the word of the Pope.

John McNeill's story unfolded over these same disconcerting years, and his biography evinces the tug and pull within an oftentimes cruel organization. His first book was published, but in 1978, John Paul II demanded he be silenced, forbidden to write or teach on the topic of homosexuality. Faithful Jesuit McNeill retreated in loyal obedience for nine years. But the system was not working for the people. Finally, in irrepressible protest of the Vatican's 1986 "Letter to the Bishops," which deemed homosexuality "an objective disorder" and called for the suppression of gay ministries, McNeill spoke out again. His religious community, the Society of Jesus, the Jesuits—his "brothers," with whom he had vowed his life—summarily dismissed him. Sadly, I lament, I have frequently seen such unjust and inhumane treatment in the Catholic Church. What a hypocritically self-serving organization at its heights! Committed to his calling, through counseling, writing, and lecturing, John continued his ministry to homosexual people; and with his life partner, Charlie Chiarelli, he supported and maintained a simple and sometimes penurious private life. A prophet not without honor except among his own—demeaned, rejected, mistreated, ridiculed, abused—John has been a living martyr to the cause of honesty and realism about human sexuality.

When he published his autobiography and, honest throughout, admitted to visiting gay haunts and to having a lover while still in the priesthood, letters to the *National Catholic Reporter* denounced this pioneer. Yet how could he have done the work he did and forge new paths for sexual minorities unless he had explored his own sexuality? Bound by the rules for Catholic priests, he could never have broken out of sexual repression—which, apparently, is what the Vatican considers virtue. Indeed, what room does the Vatican equation *sex=procreation* leave for any Catholic to become sexually integrated? Those of us who have grappled with these issues understand them fully well. A profoundly new understanding of human sexuality is emerging in our day, and it calls for courageous, if careful, response.

Of course, these notions—sexual exploration, integration, minorities—are new. They were not part of the Catholic or any Christian perspective when John published *The Church and the Homosexual*. Addressing the issues required taking new approaches. There could be no way to deal with the new information within the limits of the old understandings. I submit that John was a hero to do what he did.

My mentor Bernard Lonergan, SJ, distinguished minor and major authenticity. Minor authenticity is obedience to what you were taught; it is doing your duty faithfully as required; it is living your life within the tradition as inherited. Such authenticity maintains the status quo, and it does merit respect. In contrast, however, major authenticity goes beyond an inherited tradition. It questions, purifies, transforms, and renews the tradition. It advances the tradition along the genuine path of its inherent unfolding. Much like post-conventional morality in Lawrence Kohlberg's scheme, major authenticity is the quality of a rare few. The "greats" of all ages—including the saints—were people of major authenticity; they changed their worlds for the better. They took the tradition, dug into its core, applied it creatively, and opened for others in new circumstances a path to richer life. They are the good and faithful servants of the Gospel who bring out from their treasure both what is new and what is old (Matthew 13:52).

The challenge of major authenticity, however, is that there exists no way to judge its novelty on the spot. This is so both for the brave innovator and for the abundant critics. The innovator takes the greater risk by relying on hard-won understanding and sincere good will, trusting only the illusive Holy Spirit poured out in human hearts (Romans 5:5). Moving into uncharted territory, it ever remains to be seen where the trek beyond current boundaries will lead. Only history can judge whether major innovation is for good or ill; only history can discern whether the innovator's drive was truly authenticity.

On my reckoning, history has already moved on sufficiently to make a judgment in John McNeill's case: He was a pioneer, an explorer, a truth-seeker; he has made an incalculable contribution to religious society. The naysayers never could or would admit as much. They live in a different psychic space; they operate on a lower level of moral reasoning. It takes generations for the wisdom of the seers to color the thinking of the masses. Nonetheless, the past thirty years have more than confirmed the accuracy of the direction John took. In painful and costly service to a truth greater than himself, John McNeill opened Christian sexual ethics to third-millennium realities.

I say he is not merely a pioneer. I say he is a saint. And I use this term in its literal sense within the Catholic tradition.

Of course, he will not be canonized, certainly not in our day. Current Church leaders are incapable of recognizing the wonder of God's unfolding work among us in sexual ways.

Oh, but what of the future? What of a time when the wisdom John forged finally pervades all the church and society? And it will. It certainly will, or the church will shrivel into a curious irrelevance. What, when humanity looks back to John McNeill as a creative source of new freedom in sexual ethics and learns to prize the richness of intimate human relationships in many configurations? What, when humanity's appreciation of the beauty and diversity of God's creation advances another step or two and we are genuine enough to recognize the goodness of Christ in all the members of his body? What, when we finally grok that love is all that matters and all else—including biology—is ultimately at its service?

The life and work of John McNeill are controversial because they are innovative and far-reaching. Besides, they deal with a topic that, ironically, Incarnation-touting Christianity has yet to face squarely: sexuality. But we work and hope for the day when John's contribution will be recognized. Then others, like me now, will feel and express profound gratitude to John McNeill for the freedom, glorious freedom, that, at great cost to himself, he has offered to us all.

Daniel Helminiak teaches psychology and spirituality as Professor at the University of West Georgia. He is also a psychotherapist, Catholic priest and theologian, author, and lecturer. He holds a PhD in psychology from The University of Texas at Austin and a PhD in theology from Andover Newton Theological School and Boston College, where he was teaching assistant to Prof. Bernard Lonergan, whom Newsweek magazine called the Thomas Aquinas of the 20th Century. He is certified as a Fellow of the American Association of Pastoral Counselors and is licensed as a Professional Counselor in the state of Georgia. His book, *What the Bible Really Says about Homosexuality* (Alamo Square Press, 1994, 2000), is an international best-seller. His more recent popular books are *Spirituality for Our Global Community: Beyond Traditional Religion to a World at Peace* (2008), *The Transcended Christian: Spiritual Lessons for the Twenty-First Century* (2007), *Sex and the Sacred: Gay Identity and Spiritual Growth* (2006), and *Meditation without Myth: What I Wish They'd Taught Me in Church about Prayer, Meditation, and the Quest for Peace* (2005).

Honoring John McNeill
Pioneer, Teacher and Prophet

By
John Stasio

W hen my community at Easton Mountain honored John McNeill with our first "spiritual pioneer" award, I was reminded of how John's ministry had touched me personally and struck too by the enormity of this man's gifts to the GLBT community.

Spiritual pioneers both dare to tread were others will not go; and reinterpret the signs so that other travelers may successfully make the journey in his wake. For gay and lesbian spiritual seekers John has been a guide of invaluable support. In both of these ways John's work has been most helpful to me on my journey and in the lives of many queer spiritual seekers.

I heard of John during my years of study at Boston College. It was a personally very challenging time. I struggled to make sense of my awakening sexuality, the spiritual stirring of what I thought was a call to religious life, membership in a student community committed to peace and justice, and a curious

intellect. Dignity was the spiritual community, where my
soul was nourished, a community which owed much to John
McNeill. My spiritual director at the time, Sebastian Moore,
suggested John's books; they provided a firm intellectual
level of support for making sense out of being both queer
and Catholic.

But it was some years later that I was given, Freedom
Glorious Freedom, which I count, as one of the most influential
books in my life. The counsel on discernment was, to a gay
man who takes his spiritual life seriously, essential and life
giving. The call to spiritual maturity and the responsibility
of following one's own conscience is perhaps the greatest
gift and challenge that a teacher can offer. John offered
both. Breaking the dependency that enslaves us to perceived
authority is, in the case of gay people, a life-giving gift of
paramount significance. John McNeill pointed the way to
freedom for me and countless others. So it is with profound
respect and love that I join you in honoring John a pioneer,
teacher and prophet.

John Stasio is the founder and spiritual director of Easton
Mountain, an interfaith retreat center and spiritual community of
gay men. John was a member of the Jesuit Urban Center's Urban
Ministry team where he provided spiritual direction and bodywork
to people living with HIV/ AIDS. He is a former seminarian and
member of the Catholic Worker Community. He splits his time
between sharing a home with his partner and a golden retriever
in Albany and retreating to a cabin in the woods of Easton
Mountain.

John McNeill
Gay Love—A Holy Love

By
Brendan Fay

History is rarely linear—there is the flow and ebb of our journeys and lives personal and communal. My connection with John McNeill goes back to the late '70s and early '80s in Ireland. It was an extraordinary era in Ireland and a time of openness with the flourishing of new movements. Hope was in the air. Some focused on contemplative prayer like Taize, others on action for justice and end to nuclear weapons. Women sought equality. Catholics in the North marched for civil rights. There were vigils in solidarity with the people of El Salvador and against apartheid. In Irish villages and towns lay women and men in Charismatic prayer groups mingled with nuns and priests, read scripture with new eyes, prayed for a rebirth of the Holy Spirit and joyfully envisioned a renewed church. I was a youth leader in the Charismatic Renewal movement leading retreats and writing a column. At the same time I sought healing for my sinful condition of homosexuality. I went to regular confession. I was prayed over. For a while I had a girlfriend. A monk in Melifont gave comfort saying he suffered from the same affliction as I but asked that I remember daily I am made in the image and likeness of God. Yet in between prayers for healing and deliverance I visited the gay Hirschfield center and sought other gay men in Dublin bars. I learned too well the double life of a closeted self hating Catholic gay Irishman. An invitation for graduate studies in NY provided possible cover and escape.

In the early eighties I was a lay student of theology at St. Patrick's College, Maynooth. A moral theology course "The language and Expression of Sexual love" listed as essential reading John McNeill's *The Church and The Homosexual* along with writings of Pope John Paul II, Sebastian Moore, Jack Dominion, Edward Schillebeeckx in the section dealing with homosexuality. While I was not receptive or open seeds of hope were sown and would be recalled in another time and place years down the road. I certainly had no idea then how much our lives would eventually become entwined.

There is something about an encounter with John McNeill that is exciting, captivating and unnerving. He is like a burly bearded fisherman from the west of Ireland or a modern John the Baptist. He is both wild man and wise elder. With Jesuit confrere Dan Berrigan he was herald for peace and non violence in the midst of war, for compassion for sexual minorities and an end to divisions. He proclaimed hope in the face of despair and awakened others beyond silence and paralysis.

Whether at a kitchen table, on a plane, subway car, and in his homilies and retreats John is a constant storyteller and yet each telling is as refreshing as before—whether stories of his days as a prisoner of war in Nazi Germany and the kindness of strangers, the early days of lesbian and gay liberation or the stories from the Gospel such as the healing of the Roman Centurion's *pais*. He always returns to a few basics close to his heart—God's love for all humanity especially those who suffer injustice or live on the margins, human sexuality as gift, gay love as holy love, the invitation to become authentic, confident trust in the Holy Spirit and the unique place of the gay, lesbian, bisexual, transgender persons in the Church and world. He impresses with his theological breadth and depth. He inspires some and frustrates others with his spirit of hope and trust. His scholarly books and articles, translated in numerous languages, reflect his brilliant mind and wise heart. He is priest, preacher, and counselor and community elder. He is a man of great and profound faith. There is a tenderness to the man easily felt is his warm and welcoming embrace. While serious as psychotherapist and theologian he lightens up with a glass of wine and easily laughs and sings. And with his beloved Charles Chiarelli he is a wonderful spouse and lover delighting to speak of the joyful gift of their relationship, forty three years a growing.

Yet there is a paradox about the man who is as humble and humanly vulnerable as the next, as simple and yet complex. He is not afraid to acknowledge his doubts, moments of darkness, fears and vulnerabilities and yet is as full of conviction and determined faith as when a newly professed Jesuit. He is at once traditional and radical, holding together visions of Church past and future He has been honored for his ecumenical and universal impact. He draws easily from biblical scholarship, Maurice Blondel the subject of his dissertation from Louvain, social sciences, the arts, theology, writings of saints and popular culture. He is at home with stories of the saints, the rosary, theological debates, presiding at Eucharistic liturgies, leading retreats, at a pride parade or a demonstration for peace, a rally for equal rights.

It has been both gift and challenge over the past few years to work on a documentary about John McNeill currently entitled *Uncommon Jesuit*. I crisscrossed the US and Canada from the streets of New York to the quiet hills of Easton Mountain and Gethsemane Abbey—from Fordham University to LGBT communities on the margins of the Church in search of his story, exploring his life and legacy. Interviewing theologians, bishops, fellow Jesuits, activists, critics and admirers I trace his eighty three year old story: his Irish childhood in Buffalo, his experience as prisoner of war, life as a Jesuit theologian and university professor, the 1972 founding of Dignity, the publication in 1976 of *The Church and the Homosexual* and eventual silencing and condemnation of his public ministry to lesbian and gay people by Vatican officials. When Cardinal Joseph Ratzinger issued the October 1986 letter to Bishops on the "Pastoral Care of Homosexuals" defining gay and lesbian persons in terms such as "objective disorder" and "intrinsic evil" and Dignity communities were expelled from Catholic parishes. It was a time of pain, anger and abandonment. It was a trial of tears. John McNeill decided to break the the silence which he had endured for nine years and was expelled from his Jesuit community. Since then he has been a tireless spiritual guide and advocate for equality for the lgbt community. There is no retirement for John McNeill. In the evening of his life he continues his outreach—writing and speaking on sexuality and spirituality. It is with a deep sense of respect and affection I write of five insights from his life.

THEOLOGY AT THE SERVICE OF HUMANITY.

When published in 1976 *The Church and the Homosexual* became a multi-translated classic and marked a watershed moment in the theology of sexuality. Drawing on biblical scholarship, understandings of conscience and sexuality John revisited and called for reform of the Church's teaching and pastoral ministry with gay and lesbian persons. This was the 1970's in the wake of Stonewall and Vatican 11. It was a time of hope. John was voice of hope. Inspired by the spirit of Vatican Council he urged bishops and Church leaders to read the sign of the times, listen to the spirit in the experience of the gay and lesbian faithful and consider the *sensus fidelium*. He reminded the gay community that magisterium never replaces the inner voice of conscience, the inner voice of the Spirit in our hearts. His pioneering book was rare and among a handful on homosexuality. His theological expertise and ministry was at the service of his suffering brothers and sisters. He opened a dialogue that continues today.

John was a force for good in the Church. He called for an end to the structured injustice against lesbian and gay Christians especially when based on misinterpretations of scripture, prejudice and blind adherence to primitive understandings of sexuality. His message was profound and simple—recalled by Robert Carter SJ "it was not simply ok to be gay it was good to Gay." His work first completed in

1972 eventually received the *imprimi potest* (permission to publish), was both praised and eventually recommended by his peers including now Cardinal Avery Dulles and the saintly Jesuit superior Pedro Arrupe. Following publication in 1976 John was in much demand as an international presenter and speaker. For the gay community he was a modern day Moses. His message was ""gay love could be a holy love." Sexual expression between persons of same or opposite gender ought be judged equally. Today this remains a radical concept. For many gay catholics it was from John McNeill they first heard this "good news." He preached a message of God's inclusive love and that God's will was for each gay and lesbian person to become fully alive. He called for end to their silence, oppression and second class status.

With the backing and prayerful support of his sister Sheila from her convent in upstate New York he came out publicly as a gay man on the Today Show in front of millions of viewers. We can hardly imagine the impact. Letters came from around the world. His insights for pastoral ministry and counsel was sought. In 1977 letters also came from Rome. Because of his book and public ministry which called for reform of the Roman Catholic Church's teaching on homosexuality John was censured and silenced and by Vatican officials. He agreed and waited in patience and in hope.

FUNDING DIGNITY, COMMUNITIES OF HOSPITALITY.

When I arrived in New York in the mid eighties to study theology at St. John's University I began reading John McNeill, Carter Heyward, Mary Hunt, Jeannine Gramick,

Dan Maguire, John Boswell and Audre Lorde. I was directed to Dignity a community for gay and lesbian Catholics who gathered weekly for liturgy at St Francis Xavier a Jesuit parish in Manhattan. There were bible reflections, retreats, socials, ministry to the housebound, those in prison, the homeless. I was in amazed to hear of the genesis of this community 1972. Robert Carter, John McNeill other members of the Jesuit community of 98th street along with lay leaders affirmed and nurtured a lay led movement where persons could BE gay or lesbian and Catholic, an informed laity to renew the Church in its understanding of human sexuality. Documents, letters and stories point to the key role John played in the formation of Dignity chapters across the nation. He provided the theological garden that enabled a flourishing movement. Within a few years gay and lesbian catholics gathered weekly in homes and in Churchs for Eucharist and ministries of hospitality to pray, play and to protest injustice and violence.

As psychotherapist and counselor John also knew too well the pain of isolation and the human need for faith communities of friendship and solidarity. For it is there that faith grows and authentic healing takes place. Joining civil rights advocates early leaders soon took the message of hope from behind closed doors to the streets. John and others priests by their own courageous example risked censure and ecclesial career by walking in annual Pride parades, marching for civil rights and speaking with the media. In hope and confidence a new conversation was beginning, hearts and minds were converted. John's intuition then was that new theological insights would not emerge from intellectual debates but rather begin from the lived experience of the faithful. The Church needed to welcome, listen, embrace and honor the lives of lesbian and gay persons. John was a featured speaker at universities, local parishes and national conventions. Today he is revered internationally as a founder and father of the gay catholic civil rights movement.

HEALING AND ENCOUNTERING A GOD OF LOVE.

Since the late 60's John has ministered as priest, spiritual guide and psychotherapist during very painful days for gay, lesbian, bisexual and transgender Catholics. As priest and pastor he helped bring many back from despair, suicide, and homophobia to a place of acceptance and joy. He blessed their unions and homes. At the Blanton Peale Institute he mentored clergy, therapists and ministers. For over twenty five years men and women from across the world made their way to John's retreats at Kirkridge in rural Pennsylvania. They came to hear a word of hope, to experience healing of their broken hearts and souls, to be helped on their life journeys. He accompanied brothers and sisters through the dark night of the soul—whether victims of discrimination, crippled by homophobic fear or self hate, or suffering from addiction. John's gentle affirming, listening, healing helped unbind and set free. More importantly he opened pathways to a God of love and to resources within and among themselves. People returned year after year. At retreats he gently encouraged participants to share their own stories, to grow beyond passivity to mature autonomy, beyond victimhood to adult faith as sons and daughters of a loving God. He blessed them, sending them home as wounded healers to become agents of change in their families, churches and communities.

I interviewed John for the feature documentary on Mychal Judge, Franciscan Fire Chaplain who died in the World Trade Center on 9/11. Mychal had given copies of John's books to gay and lesbian persons and their parents who had come to him for counsel. In 1987 on a Phil Donoghue show with John as part of a panel on gay priests Mychal Judge stood up in the audience to acknowledge the unique and prophetic contribution of John McNeill. Mychal was speaking for many gay priests and brothers whom John helped to reconcile their ministry and gay humanity as sons of God.

Action on behalf Justice-Hope

John is also a man of praxis/action—action on behalf of the Gospel.

The honeymoon era of the early civil rights movement was short lived. Violence and discrimination against gays and lesbians increased. The rhetoric of hate and fear was widespread. Catholics joined the movement for civil rights. In the midst of the AIDS crisis and epidemic John witnessed the anguish, suffering and death of many friends and members of Dignity community. Along with Franciscan Mychal Judge and Patrick Kowalski John established the Upper Room Aids ministry in Harlem as an outreach to homeless persons with AIDS. Today this work continues as Harlem United. Again John taught by example refusing to be silent. Where many had given up on hope for reform. Like a voice in the wilderness, he was a lone prophet of hope speaking truth to power whether ecclesial or societal. His struggles of conscience and conflicts with Jesuit superiors and Vatican officials. Then in October 1986 the letter from Rome resulted in Dignity communities were expelled out. Priests were ordered to end their ministry.

In 1987 McNeill was expelled from the Jesuit community because of his outspoken ministry and refusal to be silent. He did not look back. He did not give in to despair. But With Charlie at his side he looked to the future with hope. Despite all he has been through with John there is no self pity or bitterness. He is to this day a man of patient waiting and expectant trust. He reflects the words of Belgian Cardinal Leo Suenens "Happy Are those who dream dreams and are ready to pay the price to make them come true." For John there is a balance between the reflective journey inward and the journey outward from the closet and into the streets. Gay liberation is not a mere personal affair. By faith all are the agents of change in the Church and in the world around us, to be light and salt.

GAY LOVE—A HOLY LOVE

John says he would not have been able to write and speak on homosexuality or gay love without the experience of love between he and Charlie. In the early days Charlie was often the quiet supporting life partner to John who continued to live out his call and ministry. Indeed John would be the first to say that Charlie is as much part of his ministry and that his books are a witness to their life of shared love. As feminist theologian Mary Hunt wrote, with Charlie John became "honest in love." For many Catholic gay men in a church that continues to decry same sex love and tenderness as intrinsic evil and objective disorder they became models of good and healthy loving and mentors of personal maturing. Their love is a light that shines warmly.

Rather than keeping silent whenever John speaks he honors Charlie. His very honesty is a gift. He broke the fierce code of clerical silence, the ecclesial don't ask, don't tell. The chosen path of honesty has cost many their career and life. Homophobia, heterosexism diminishes not just the lives of individual gay men and lesbians who serve in schools, parishes and communities but the very life of the whole Church. With respect and sensitivity John has helped many walk the joyful but challenging path of greater honesty and openness. John helped usher in an era of honesty where religious orders could speak about their gay priests and lesbian nuns, where parishes and families could acknowledge the gifts of their gay sons and lesbian daughters. He has helped free and liberate men and women from the duplicitous yoke of the closet and discover love and sexual joy for the first time. John and Charlie in their very togetherness as a committed couple invite us to be good lovers of one another. Whether straight or queer, celibate, single or married, priest, bishop, religious or lay the witness of John and Charlie is to love well and live well. John and Charlie are respected elders in the LGBT community. They are men of extraordinary faith and courage.

In April 2005 as Joseph Cardinal Ratzinger was becoming Benedict xvi in Rome a New York based Irish LGBT group Lavender & Green Alliance gathered to honor John with The Roger Casement—Eva Gore Booth Leadership Award. The celebration called *Oiche Aerach* X (Gaelic for Gay Night). Surprising many John unembittered and with characteristic hope urged those gathered not to despair or abandon the faith but to welcome the new Pope and to trust the Holy Spirt at work. Pointing to the recent vote in Spain to extend civil marriage to same sex couples he noted we live in good if challenging times He urged all to trust their own conscience and experience as lesbian gay bisexual transgender people and to work for justice and equality. Our era could mark the end of dependence on patriarchal leadership and open doors for a more inclusive church. Concluding his reflection he then turned towards Charlie embraced him and thanked him for his committed love of 40 years.

It was particularly joyful to be a legal witness for John and Charlie for their Civil Marriage on September 8 2008 in Toronto where they first met New Years eve 1965. Friends and family who traveled from the U.S. and Canada clapped and shed tears of joy as Judge Harvey Brownstone Canada's first openly gay judge concluded the ceremony and declared John and Charlie legally married spouses. John's ring is inscribed "Taking a Chance on God" (a title of one of his books) and Charlie's intimately penned, "Taking a Chance on Jack." John and Charlie's civil marriage is a legal recognition and affirmation of what they have lived for over four decades since they first set eyes and hearts on each other. It's ironic that in 2008 pioneers of the gay civil rights movement in the U.S. had to travel from their home state of Florida to Canada for the simple right to marry. John and Charlie's long-awaited legal marriage is the fruit of their life's labor. I am glad they live to celebrate the human joy of being newlyweds and a legally married couple.

That night like a mantra John repeated what he has said for four decades "The love between Charlie and me is a holy love and a sharing in divine love."

With Charlie by his side, with confidence in God—John McNeill has hope for the future and trusting the Holy Spirit within us and among us, leading us into truth.

So with affection I join in honoring the life of our brother, father and friend John McNeill—a life unceasing in love of the Gospel, contemplative trust, listening and compassion for a broken humanity and action on behalf of justice and equality.

With him we look forward and work passionately for the day when exclusion and discrimination will be history and our church will be a place where all Gods people are welcomed openly, where committed love gay and straight will be blessed, supported and affirmed as good and holy!

Brendan Fay is a Catholic activist and filmmaker. He holds BA and MA degrees in theology from St. Patrick's College, Maynooth, Ireland and St. John's University in New York. He is founder and co-chair of New York's inclusive St. Patrick's Parade and founder of Lavender and Green Alliance serving the needs of the Irish LGBT community. He is a regular presenter on gay spirituality and marriage at churches, colleges, rallies and retreats. He has testified in Dublin, Warsaw, Washington, and New York. He has been arrested several times for civil rights.

He directed "A Month's Mind" and was co-producer of "Saint of 9/11" highly praised films about Mychal Judge, the Franciscan Fire chaplain who died in the World Trade Center attack on 9/11.

Fay has been involved in the movement for marriage equality since 1998 and is co-chair of the Civil Marriage Trail Project bringing couples across the borders to Canada and Massachusetts for legal marriage. He is editing an anthology entitled "Same Sex Marriage: Catholic Conversations." Brendan lives in Astoria NY with his spouse Tom Moulton. They were among the first binational couples to legally marry in Canada in July 2003. Their wedding was the subject of an Irish TV documentary.

He can reached at : Brendan@stpatsforall.com

Brendan Fay is producing a documentary on the life and ministry of John McNeill. "Uncommon Jesuit" premieres in early 2009.

THE REAL THING
A LETTER TO READERS

BY

TROY PERRY

Father John McNeill is the real thing! He has lived out his life completely with integrity and as an out and open gay man as a Jesuit in the Roman Catholic Church.

This new book is a companion to the documentary that is being released about this saint of God. You will not want to miss purchasing this book. Father John McNeill continues to be one of the prophetic voices that continues to call we who are part of the Lesbian, Gay, Bi-, and Transgendered community back to our faith in God.

The Reverend Troy Perry, American minister and activist, born; founded the Metropolitan Community Church, a Christian denomination with a special affirming ministry with the LGBT communities, in Los Angeles on October 6, 1968. In 1968, after a suicide attempt following a failed love affair, and witnessing a close friend being arrested by the police in a Gay bar, Perry felt called to return to his faith and to offer a place for Gay people to worship God freely. The MCC has become a major Christian denomination with churches all around the world.

About John J. McNeill

John J. McNeill is a psychotherapist, a moral theologian, teacher, scholar, writer and lecturer and has had many articles published in numerous journals, magazines and books.

John J. McNeill and Charlie Chiarelli were legally married Monday September 8, 2008 in Toronto where they first met nearly 43 years before.

McNeill can be reached at jjmcneill@aol.com

Also of interest from
Lethe Press and White Crane Books

A Prophet in His Own Land: A Malcolm Boyd Reader
edited by Bo Young and Dan Vera

Take Off the Masks
Malcolm Boyd

Someone Gay
Don Clark, Ph.D.

ALL: A James Broughton Reader
edited by Jack Foley

Gay Spirit: Myth and Meaning
Mark Thompson

Two Flutes Playing
Andrew Ramer

Gay Spirituality
Toby Johnson

Gay Perspective
Toby Johnson

lethepressbooks.com   whitecranebooks.org

DIOCESAN RESOURCE CENTER
1551 TENTH AVENUE EAST
SEATLE, WA 98102-0126

Breinigsville, PA USA
02 February 2011
254683BV00002B/80/P